The
Fortune Teller's
Handbook

The Fortune Teller's Handbook

A fun way to discover your future

SASHA FENTON

A Sterling/Zambezi Book
Sterling Publishing Company, Inc.
New York

Dedication

To the memory of my friend Gordon A. Smith, who has given me so much advice on psychic matters over the years.

Acknowledgments

A big thank you to all those who offered information and advice in connection with some of the chapters.
Another big thank you to Nigel Bourne for the illustrations in the runes and numerology chapters.

Library of Congress Cataloging-in-Publication Data Available

10 9 8 7 6 5 4 3 2 1

Published in 2003 by Sterling Publishing Co., Inc.
387 Park Avenue South, New York, NY 10016

First published in 2002 by Zambezi Publishing
©2002 Sasha Fenton
Distributed in Canada by Sterling Publishing
^c/o Canadian Manda Group, One Atlantic Avenue, Suite 105
Toronto, Ontario, Canada M6K 3E7
Distributed in Australia by Capricorn Link (Australia) Pty. Ltd.
P.O. Box 704, Windsor, NSW 2756 Australia

Sterling ISBN 1-4027-0481-X

Disclaimer

This book will be on sale in many countries around the world, and sadly, it is a fact of life nowadays that there are a few people around who try to get rich by harassing others where one law or another leaves a loophole, so there is a parallel need to avoid such problems. The alternative would be never to write nonfiction books at all!

This book is designed to provide information in regard to the subject matter covered. It is sold with the understanding that the publisher and the author are not engaged in rendering legal, accounting, advisory or any other professional services in this book, and cannot be held responsible for the outcome if any of the contents are used for any purpose whatsoever. If expert assistance is required in connection with any subject matter covered within this book, the services of a competent professional should be sought.

It is not the purpose of this book to reprint all the information that is otherwise available to the author and/ or publisher, but to complement, amplify and supplement other texts. You are urged to read all the available material, learn as much as possible about the subject matter and to tailor the information to your individual needs.

Fortune telling is not a get-rich-quick scheme. Anyone who decides to make a career out of the application of any divinatory systems must expect to invest a lot of time, effort and resources. Also, the spiritual aspect of such work ensures that it should never be seen solely in terms of moneymaking.

Every effort has been made to make this book as complete and accurate as possible within the limitations of size and content. However, there may be mistakes, both typographical and in content. Therefore, this text should be used only as a general guide and not as an ultimate source of data on the subject matter concerned. Furthermore, only information known to the author and/or publisher up to the printing date is included.

The purpose of this book is to educate and entertain. The author and/or publisher shall have neither liability nor responsibility to any person or entity with respect to any loss or damage caused, or alleged to be caused, directly or indirectly by the information contained in this book.

If you do not wish to be bound by the above, you may return this book to the publisher for a full refund.

Contents

INTRODUCTION

Men and women have visited fortune tellers of one kind or another since the dawn of time. Even the most skeptical person enjoys an occasional reading, while many others visit a consultant at least once a year. There are hundreds of different methods of fortune telling, which range from highly developed skills to methods that simply prod the divinator's psychic awareness. A professional psychic knows how to get the best from his spiritual guides because he has spent years studying and training in psychic development. A skilled astrologer, palmist, numerologist etc. is not really a fortune teller at all, but a combination of map-reader, mathematician, and psychoanalyst. Not everyone however, wishes to devote his or her life to this kind of training; many people just want the fun and insight of being able to tell someone's fortune by a simple method of prediction. This book investigates a number of different methods, all of them easy to understand and to use, as a means of introducing you to the mysteries of these ancient crafts. In some cases, there are full-sized books available on the divination in question, while others are too old-fashioned or unusual to be taken seriously, but even where these are concerned, you might find something more about them on the Internet.

Where necessary I have drawn information for the divinations with which I am less familiar from other professionals. I hope this brings these subjects to life and shows the reality of working in these fields rather than simply explaining the theories behind the methods. Where the information has come from other Readers, I have given them full acknowledgement for their contributions. I have used a variety of terms such as Questioner, Enquirer, Querent, Reader, Sitter, and Consultant in this book because all these terms are in common use. I have mainly used the masculine terms "he" and "him" in order to keep the text simple. Fortune tellers and their clients are masculine, feminine, gay, straight, old, young, rich, poor, and from every country and culture in the world.

NUMEROLOGY

This ancient method of divination is one of those that can be taken on a super-ficial level or it can be looked at very deeply. Numerology, like astrology, will give a good deal of information about a person's character as well as being helpful in predicting the pattern of trends and tendencies for the future. It is fascinating to work out and look at in the context of one's lifestyle at any given period of time. The numerologist Fred Curtis helped by giving me some useful information for this chapter.

The character of a name

The letters of your name need to be translated into a number system. Some numerologists insist that the name on a person's birth certificate should be used, but very few people use their name in that form. In my opinion it makes more sense to use the name that you are happy and comfortable with than one your parents chose for you, and the name that you actually use should resonate properly with the person you are now. If you use a different name for your professional life than the one you use at home, try both and see what results you get.

The Alphabet Code

1	2	3	4	5	6	7	8	9
A	B	C	D	E	F	G	H	I
J	K	L	M	N	O	P	Q	R
S	T	U	V	W	X	Y	Z	

Count up the numbers in your whole name including any middle name that you use. Once you have done this, reduce the name to one digit. This will show you your basic character. Your soul urge is shown by the vowels while the per-sonality that you show to the outside world is shown by the consonants.

Example:
L I N D A   T U L L E Y
3 9 5 4 1   2 3 3 3 5 7

Full name

Total numbers:	= 45
Reduction: 4 + 5	= 9

Therefore Linda Tulley is a 9.

Vowels—soul urge

I A U E
9 1 3 5

Total numbers:	= 18
Reduction: 1 + 8	= 9

Consonants—life lesson

L N D T L L Y
3 5 4 2 3 3 7

Total numbers:	= 27
Reduction: 2 + 7	= 9

Linda Tulley therefore, has much the same feelings inside as those that she shows to the world. Her inner desires and her daily requirements are the same. She is an uncomplicated lady and she has reached a comfortable stage in her evolution.

Here is an example of someone far more complex:

Full name

F R A N K A N D E R S O N
6 9 1 5 2 1 5 4 5 9 1 6 5

Total numbers:	= 59
Reduction: 5 + 9	= 14
Reduction: 1 + 4	= 5

Vowels—soul urge

A A E O
1 1 5 6

Total numbers:	= 13
Reduction: 1 + 3	= 4

Consonants—life lesson

F R N K N D R S N
6 9 5 2 5 4 9 1 5

Total numbers:	= 46
Reduction: 4 + 6	= 10
Reduction: 1 + 0	= 1

Frank projects an outward appearance of confidence and competence due to his consonant (1) while being basically a mercurial person who has many interests and a need to communicate (5). He is reaching for security, a logical routine and method to his life and a reliable inner world of stable relationships and finances that make some kind of realistic sense to him (4).

Naturally, there is more to numerology than this. Each letter has a value according to its position in the alphabet. An A for instance is more important than an E or an O.

The destiny number

The birth date shows the *destiny* for each person. It is also the birth date, in conjunction with any specific month or year, that is used for predicting trends and events.

Example one

Linda Tulley: July 17, 1946

| Reduction: 7 + 1 + 7 + 1 + 9 + 4 + 6 | = 35 |
| Reduction: 3 + 5 | = 8 |

Linda's life lesson is to cope with a structured and organized lifestyle that doesn't leave much time for personal freedom or pleasure. Poor Linda. The fact is that Linda is the wife of a successful businessman who works in the construction trade. She helps him a little with the paperwork but she is also fully occupied with her job as a registered nanny. She has four sons, and she is the first to admit that her fourth pregnancy was not planned and that her life is extremely busy and highly structured. Linda occasionally resents the fact that she rarely gets to leave her large house and that she has little time for herself.

Example two

Frank Anderson: March 3, 1935

| Reduction: 3 + 2 + 7 + 1 + 9 + 3 + 5 | = 30 |
| Reduction: 3 + 0 | = 3 |

Frank's life lesson is to have the courage to grow and develop in a creative manner, also to cope with success and material gain. However, Frank's soul urge being a highly structured 4 makes this hard for him. He needs fun, humor and to be able to own and enjoy things of value without feeling guilty. He needs to develop sensitivity and to control the more obstinate or awkward sides of his personality.

THE CHARACTER OF EACH NUMBER

Start by taking the number in the whole name for an overview of a person's character, and then look at their soul urge and life lesson numbers. In the case of our example of Frank Anderson, this would mean checking out the numbers 5, 4 and 1.

Number One

The number one relates to the self and also to the conscious, rational, reasoning mind. Any achievement needs to be preceded by a thought before it can be translated into action. The number one stands alone. It is bold, powerful, and it is a force that translates energy into matter. It has strongly masculine qualities. This number is pioneering, the first in line, dominant, original and independent. The downside is that this leads to domineering and selfish behavior that can easily turn to aggression. It is wonderful when this person uses his powers of invention to get things done, to better himself to help others and to protect those he loves. However, if he uses it to bully others, he won't get very far in love or working relationships.

This number shows that the person may have been dominated and bullied as a child. One or both parents may have thought they were always right, possibly due to their religious beliefs. They put pressure upon the youngster to perform or conform to their ideal. The upside of this is that the subject turns into a hard working and ambitious type who is especially suited to self-employment or to reaching the top in a profession. The downside is that the number one person may copy his parents' pattern and seek to dominate others in his turn. Alternatively, he may become anxious and fearful of the future. If he can find someone who will love him and give him the emotional support that he needs, he can overcome this. He would not only become successful in life, but others would value him for his honesty, generosity, humor and sense of adventure.

Number Two

This number implies duality. It represents the womb-like quality of nurturing a seed that has been planted by the number one energy. It represents a drive for harmony and balance, a need for a feminine yin to balance the masculinity of yang. It is passive, intuitive, receptive and emotional. This number indicates partnerships and relationships, so the chances are that these will be important to the person.

There may have been considerable tensions in the childhood home, and this leads this person to develop a hard shell in order to protect himself. Childhood events may result in the kind of insecurity that he relieves by becoming penny-pinching and miserly. He may seek to acquire goods in order to make himself feel safe. Even if he doesn't go to this extreme, he will probably always be careful with money and possessions. He is very keen on family life and he will be fiercely loyal to his loved ones, and he will even carry the habit of loyalty through to his employers. He is not a natural leader, because he prefers to help others and to be appreciated for what he does. He may choose to work in one of the caring professions.

Number Three

This is a creative number, so it represents creative enterprise and growth. The seed that was planted in a number one year and nurtured during a number two year is now showing signs of growth. This number suggests that material benefits will eventually come to this person.

This person may be quite artistic or he may have literary talents, but he may not have been encouraged to express this during his youth, so this may lead to frustration. This subject probably found it difficult to stand up to his parents and he may have a problem with authority figures throughout life. The result is that he may be stubborn and irritable when dealing with others, or too charming and accommodating. Despite a difficult start, he usually does well in his chosen profession. He may also be extremely lucky in his choice of friends and colleagues, and these people may be happy to help him whenever they can. He is sociable and flirtatious, he enjoys having a good time and also seeing others enjoy themselves.

Number Four

This number signifies the earth and the physical and the material world. It represents a foundation that a person can build upon. Number four is the number of form and it represents common sense, reason and control over the energies that are at one's command. This represents balance, stability and security, but it also symbolizes restrictions and limitations. Logical thinking and systematic work methods belong to this number.

This subject's childhood should have been a happy one with plenty of love and support from family and teachers. He may get into the habit later in life of leaning on others and treating them as replacement parents or teachers. He will always be a hard and reliable worker with a sensible attitude to whatever he takes on. He is loyal and sensitive to those he loves. He is a loyal employee, although he can also succeed in a business of his own. He may be a little unimaginative, but he makes an excellent financial advisor or craftsman, and his capacity for hard work earns rewards. He is a loyal and loving family person.

Number Five

The number five shows the need to break out of the enclosed structure that is signified in the number four. This number breeds activity because it hates routine and restriction, and it becomes very nervous and restless when held down. It hates to see its freedom threatened because it needs a wide area in which to move around and to express its drive and energy. The number five seeks constant change and variety, and the scope to put the fruits of physical and mental experiences into action. This number is associated with social contacts, education, ideas and communications of all kinds.

This person's parents were reasonable and his childhood was fairly happy, but there were events that made him feel very insecure. His parents may have been sick, they may have been refugees of some kind, or they may just have moved around a lot, which meant that the subject had to go through several changes of home or school. He may tend to walk away from problems rather than face them. His desire for the admiration of others may lead him to become a success in sports or the media. He is clever and versatile; he needs variety in his life and a number of different challenges in his job. He enjoys moving around and meeting a variety of different people in his working and social life, or talking on the phone much of the time. He accepts the ideas of others, but he can be a good leader because he allows others to do their jobs without undue interference. He cannot have a relationship with a boring partner.

Number Six

This number is associated with feelings and emotions. It also relates to the home, to family life and to the love that is received (or otherwise) from the parents. It rules the ability to give love and to care for a family. The number six represents responsibility for others and providing them with food, warmth, love and security. Number six relates to all that is beautiful and harmonious, especially in the areas of giving, caring and looking after the health of others.

This subject will have felt extremely insecure when young and he may have had parents who either did not communicate or who gave him strangely mixed messages. His mother may have had some sensible things to say at times, but also some very fixed ideas that may not have been normal or logical. His family venerated hard work and he may have sought to impress them and to win their approval by working hard—even as a child. The outcome is that he becomes a tireless worker in adult life, possibly wearing himself out for the sake of others. If his family and employers appreciate and value him for the effort that he makes, he will feel that he has achieved all that he set out to do. His chief fault is perfectionism. This subject's mind is excellent and he does much to help others, often through a genuine desire to make the world a better place to live.

Number Seven

This number represents two ideas that are linked. The first is the need for rest, relaxation and time off to think things through, or just to allow thoughts to drift around aimlessly. After a while, the thoughts take shape and something useful will emerge. The second idea is that of spiritual significance, as this encompasses the kind of reflection, analysis and inward journey that leads to enlightenment of both a practical and spiritual nature. In essence, this is a meditative number.

This person probably had a fairly easy-going relationship with parents and other adults, partly because he is reasonable, sociable and pleasant. He turns his amiable nature to good advantage both in his career and his personal relationships, but he needs to guard against a tendency to let opportunities pass him by. This subject must avoid sitting back and allowing others to make progress at his expense or to take what should rightfully be his. He prefers thinking to acting and he tends to sit back and observe the world and all that goes on there. He may become a philosopher, a mystic or an artist. He is wise but he may not cash in on his talents and wisdom or achieve much. If he can develop his artistic talents and find a practical life partner, he will find that the world appreciates him.

Number Eight

This number suggests material success but also spiritual attainment. There has to be progress in both areas and a balance needs to be maintained between them. This karmic number shows that we reap what we sow. The number eight also indicates a mastery over the physical world and an acceptance of responsibility.

If the subject's destiny number is eight, his childhood will not have been easy, either because he was rebellious and disinclined to conform, or because one or both of his parents was domineering, dictatorial or rigid. He may have dealt with this by defying his parents or by using cunning and sly behavior to get what he wanted. Either way, he learned to use charm later in life to get what he wants. He is extremely intuitive and can sum up people and situations almost in a flash. Add this to his sharp intelligence, organizational ability and capacity for hard work, and it is easy to see that he will make a tremendous success of his chosen career. He is the one who will end up with wealth and status. He may become domineering himself in later life and may see even his personal relationships as a kind of power struggle. If he can curb his sharp tongue and learn to be tolerant of those who are not lucky enough to be born with his strength and courage, he can make his loved ones happy and in turn become happy himself. He needs to ease up a little and learn to relax and enjoy life.

Number Nine

 This incorporates all the previous numbers, so it represents completion and true love of the highest order. This shows that a certain point has been reached although there are always higher levels to aspire to. Listening to our inner voices and working by divine standards are the only means to success. In this case the soul may be old but there is always something more to learn.

If the subject is a nine-destiny person, his parents were keen for him to do well and he could go on to prove them right by becoming a success. He has an inner urge for exploration, and this could take him into the realms of education or hobbies and interests that give him an opportunity to look at things from a variety of different angles. In many cases, the visionary aspect of his nature can lead to an involvement in religion, philosophy or the spiritual life, and he can inspire others. Travel is a strong theme in his life, and he could end up seeing a fair bit of the world.He uses his ability to get on with all manners of people to bring him success in business, but there is a side of his nature that could lead him to simply drift along without getting anywhere very much.

N.B.: Although numerology normally uses the numbers from one to nine, the numbers eleven, twenty-two and thirty-three are also used when assessing a person's character.

Number Eleven

The energy behind this number is of justice, fair play and of strength that is used wisely. There are times when it is right to administer justice but others when it is right just to sit back and wait things out. The trick is to know which is which.

As a destiny number, eleven suggests that the subject's childhood might have been reasonable, but something made him determined to keep himself to himself. He may have been distrustful of adults or of other children or disinclined to listen to anything that others had to say. He seems to have been a quiet and rather serious child. In later life, he could become opinionated, inflexible and difficult. He may develop a terrific inferiority complex, which he hides under an arrogant, uncaring or defiant attitude. If he finds the right career outlet for his talents and develops sensitivity towards others, he may overcome his natural tendency for self-absorption. He has an original mind and is attracted to unconventional ideas and an unconventional lifestyle. Marriage, children and a routine family life may never appeal to him.

Number twenty-two

There is an element of justice that must be applied here. He may receive just or unjust treatment during the course of his life but should always strive to be fair in his dealings with others. There is a feeling of completion here, with just rewards for all that he has done before (perhaps in a previous life).

If the subject's destiny number is twenty-two, he both loved and admired his parents or feared their strength and domination. He grew up to become an independent person with an unusual outlook or non-conformist attitude. He understands the underlying motives of others. He also has an uncanny feel for the structure of materials and this could lead him to become a builder, civil engineer, architect or creative artist. He also makes an excellent counselor and guide to younger people. If he can control his tendency towards angry or wounding outbursts, he can succeed in a relationship, especially one with a partner who needs to be guided and cared for.

Number thirty-three

This is a difficult number in which loneliness and hardship will occur, but these experiences bring enlightenment and an ability to sympathize with the plight of others. Charitable work, doing things for others and self-sacrifice have a part to play here, but there is also the development of a strong inner world of spirituality and artistry.

If this is the subject's destiny number, he may have been somewhat isolated during his childhood, possibly due to sickness and spells in the hospital, and this led him to develop him creativity and imagination. Later in life when storms threaten, he can escape into a dream world of his own making. His parents were not particularly hard on him, but life and circumstances made him a little fearful. He will probably end up in one of the caring professions. He might take up spiritual work where he spends his life helping and giving himself to others. The danger here is that he becomes overtaken by the needs of others and expends his energies, leaving him drained and exhausted. If necessary, he can be practical and very successful, but he probably will always want to help others. If he can develop his artistic talents and work quietly on his own projects, he can achieve considerable success.

o O o

PERSONAL MONTH OR YEAR FORTUNES

It is easy to discover your fortune for a particular year. All you need to do is to add the numbers of the day and month of your birth to the year as a whole. For example, if you were born on September the 2nd and you want to look at 2004, this would mean adding $9 + 2 + 2 + 0 + 0 + 4$ to make 17 which then reduces to the number 8.

If you want to look at the first four months of the year, add your *whole name* number to the year in question. For the middle four months, add the *life lesson* number, and for the last four months, add the *soul urge* number.

It is worth bearing in mind that, while a number *one* year indicates a fresh start for any person, any year or any part of a year that is the same as your destiny number is bound to be important.

A number one year

Key ideas: Beginning, initiative, decisions, individuality

This is the start of a new phase, so if you apply it to a whole year, what you do now will determine the pattern of events for the following nine years. If you apply it to a four-month period, this sets the tone for the next few months. You may feel quite alone during this year even if family and friends surround you, and you may wonder how you are going to make it on your own. You need to decide how you are going to operate your life and to make decisions that should determine your future course. This is a period in which you set things in place, although you may not be able to get them off the ground in quite the way that you would like just yet. In some ways, this is a period of adjustment in which you may find yourself coping with a new way of life.

You will feel surges of energy and a desire to do things for yourself. This may be a matter of personal choice or it may be that you find yourself alone and unsupported. You won't want to accept defeat because you will feel that your instincts are right. It would be a good idea to take time out on occasion to reflect and to listen to your intuition and also to heed sensible advice. You will find it necessary to put yourself first at this time and to set your own plans into action.

You will shed old problems and any lingering timidity will vanish. There will be new methods of work to come to grips with and new ways of looking at old problems. Important people may come into your life at this time and they may act as mentors or teachers. Be discriminating in your choice of friends at this time, because alliances that are made now will last. This is the time to stand up for what you believe in, to be self-reliant, self-motivated and independent.

A number two year

Key ideas: Cooperation, partnerships, creativity, peace, harmony, peaceful coexistence

You will need to work in harmony with others and you will need to be aware of their requirements. You may need to take a slightly passive role and to be diplomatic when handling other people. You may be called upon to judge situations on behalf of others and to settle disputes. Partnership matters will be important but so will personal creativity. You will find that you have useful flashes of inspiration.

This is not a good time to make major decisions, and if things become unstable it will be best to keep going and to remain passive while allowing things to take their course. Love affairs may become unsettled due to hidden factors and underlying problems, however you can work on these in order to improve them. You may uncover some kind of deception around you or discover secret enemies who work against you. If others are not honest with you, at least be honest with yourself. Try to take time out to relax and to tune into your own intuition, as this will be your best guide at such times.

A number three year

Key ideas: Activity, expansion, travel, creativity, self-expression

You may feel the urge to travel within your own country or overseas—either way you will feel the need to move around freely and to explore. Take the opportunity to do so, because this will prove to be a mind-broadening experience. New faces and new horizons will enable you to assess yourself in a different light.

This is a year of activity and social events in which you will make yourself the center of attention. The new exposure will make you take a fresh look at yourself and you may wish to change your image or appearance. It is important that you look good because a positive appearance and a confident manner will impress those who you come into contact with. This could be an unusually lucky period in which you may win as a result of entering competitions or even gambling. Business opportunities are also in the air now.

There may be a new baby in your circle during this period, and there will certainly be new and far more creative projects to sink your teeth into at this time. Be sure that the enthusiasm, optimism and expansion don't lead to extravagance, wastefulness and loss. Overindulgence might lead to weight gain. The domestic scene could prove troublesome, possibly because you will be busy elsewhere. If you scatter your time and energies too much, you will lose your effectiveness. If you drift along and make no effort, this could be a wasted year but if you make an effort to carry your ideas through in a constructive manner, this could be one of the happiest years of your life.

A number four year

Key ideas: Work, law and order, budgeting, foundations, sex and regeneration or recycling in some way

This is a time to concentrate on work on the material plane. You may be so determined to organize your life that you clear out the attic, cellar, cupboards, desks, drawers and the garage. You will be driven by a subconscious desire to build a firm and secure foundation, so you will tidy up your environment and put your affairs into order.

Everything relating to money and possessions will become important now and it is essential that you make your life secure and stable, so you will need to budget carefully. This number highlights land, property, building and renovations, so you could find yourself confronted with extra expense in this area of your life. Take care of your money, and it will take care of you. Your body is your home as well, so the extravagances and excesses of the previous cycle will make you keen to get back into shape. As all the physical senses become heightened, your current sexual relationship should become rewarding and stimulating. Males could decide to father children now.

This number relates to law and order so you must be sure to behave honestly in all your dealings. You may be well on the way to business success now, so this is a good time to buy material goods and possessions. Enjoy this by all means but don't become a slave to possessions—own them and don't allow them to own you. Also pay attention to the health and finances of your family. You may become stubborn and oversensitive at this time.

A number five year

Key ideas: Communication, decisions, change, experience, sexual magnetism

There is so much activity in your life at the moment that you will find it hard to keep up the pace. You are so totally involved in attending meetings, running errands, answering the telephone, making arrangements and going to parties and social functions that you feel as though you are on a merry-go-round.

This is a period of communication and education, so gaining experience and making contacts will be your most important activity now. You need to look closely at your life and to choose the right direction because change is in the air. If you are dissatisfied with your current situation, this is the time to do something about it. New doors will open to you and new solutions to your problems will present themselves.

This is the year in which the opposite sex suddenly discovers you. Your calendar will be filled, you will become the life and soul of any party and admirers will surround you. This activity will include travel, so ensure that your car is in working order and that your gas tank is full. Your nervous system will be at full stretch, so it might be advisable to avoid too much alcohol and keep away from drugs. You need to be at your best rather than under any chemical influence. You may feel that you are wasting your energies on superficial relationships, but this is probably not the time for commitment. You may need light-hearted love affairs for what they can teach you.

This is not a year for routine activities, and you will need to be free to take off at a moment's notice. Indeed, there will be several unexpected and very pleasant events. You may feel resentful towards those who seek to hold you back or keep you down, and this may encourage you to break away from stultifying relationships. Without change, there is no growth, but you still need to focus upon some underlying goal so that you don't simply fritter this year away in aimless pleasure seeking.

A number six year

Key ideas: Duty, responsibility, love, home, family, justice, beauty, emotional matters

During a number six year, the emphasis is usually on the home and family. There may be changes in the home with new people entering the family while others leave. Responsibilities within the home will increase. This year number is associated with marriage but it can also indicate divorce, and this is because you will seek a balance in this area of your life. During the restless phase of the previous year, you may have experimented with new relationships, and you may begin to feel that you are ready to cope with a settled relationship and to establish a home.

Beauty will become an issue, both in relation to your own personal appearance and also that of your surroundings. You might decorate your home and you will certainly take more care of your appearance. You are so tuned into the need for balance that you could become a peacemaker, and you could even take up counseling in a professional capacity. Some legal decisions will occur and these will also be aimed at restoring balance and harmony.

If balance cannot be restored, separations will occur and differences will become irreconcilable—either in your personal life or in the business arena. Try to settle arguments with fairness, and try to show understanding towards your loved ones during this period. This is a year of duty to others, both within the home and at work, so the only way to get anywhere is to work hard and do what has to be done.

A number seven year

Key ideas: Rest, perfection, health, analysis

This is a period of retreat. You may feel more tired than usual and you may not wish to socialize. You need time alone to think, meditate, reflect, and analyze matters and to go on an inward journey. It is a good time to take weekends off or vacations by the sea or in the countryside. Try to set material worries aside now and don't push yourself too hard. Do the work that is on hand and don't take on anything more. Leave goals and ambitions alone for a while, because if you work too hard at this time you will make yourself ill.

This is a good time to take a course of study and it may be that mind, body and spirit subjects grab your attention, as you are in a particularly receptive frame of mind at this time. You may experience interesting dreams, visions and psychic events. The fact is that you have spent the last few years getting your body, home, work, family and finances into shape, so this is a good time to take things easier and to concentrate on spiritual matters.

A number eight year

Key ideas: Karma, responsibility, strength, business, service to others, sex, balance, harmony.

Now the truth of everything becomes clear and karma reigns. The law of cause and effect will bring you what you have earned or what you deserve. For some, this means advancement in your career, a higher salary, public recognition, honor, awards and even legacies. For others there will be hardship, material loss, unemployment and possibly even bankruptcy. The emphasis will be on the more serious aspects of finance and security. Pressures and responsibilities at work will mount and you will feel the strain of the extra workload, although this may come as a result of promotion or of starting something new.

Additional money will be available and you may even receive an inheritance, so your bank balance should be healthier. However, the negative aspect could include job loss, business failure and financial burdens. Either way, pressure and responsibility become key issues.

Intense sexual relationships are possible now and this could also be wrapped up with responsibility for others. A relationship may feel like heaven on earth. Whatever the prevailing financial situation, you and your partner will pull together during this phase. If you allow the loss of material possessions to get you down and get so bent on gaining more possessions that you start to dominate others, you will become unhappy. Whatever your circumstances, a balance between the material and spiritual world will need to be found.

A number nine year

Key ideas: Endings, transition, charity, friendships, wisdom.
This is the last year of a nine-year cycle, so your fortune has turned full circle and you are almost back to the beginning again, so you are preparing for the wheel to make another revolution. If you have been operating in harmony with the universe, you will have gained much experience and knowledge over the past nine years. If your life has been out of balance, then you will have experienced loss, heartache and upheaval. Now is the time to find the right spiritual values, greater understanding, a stronger mental attitude and spiritual awareness.

This is the time to let go of worn-out values, to give up those associations that have no place in your life or future. People may leave your life, or you may change your career or relocate your home and leave some people or things to which you are attached. The status quo will be upset. If you find change and transformation difficult, this will be an emotionally trying time. You may feel like crying at times and you will need to retreat from life at times and reflect on your situation. You will come into contact with your inner self. When endings occur, it is because there is something new around the corner and when one door closes, another opens. Try to be aware of this and to accept changes willingly, because ultimately, they will be for your own good. Use some of your energies in charitable deeds, and give back to the universe some of what you have gained.

You should not try to work alone now, but join with others for the common good. Be sympathetic, compassionate, understanding and loving to those who you encounter during this cycle. Old friendships can become especially meaningful and heart-warming, while beautiful new relationships can develop.

Negatively, some people become overemotional during a number nine vibration, and they refuse to listen or even try to understand what is going on. If you try to cling to those things that you can no longer have, you simply prolong a transition period and also prolong the pain. Don't look back to past insecurities, look to the future. You cannot change the past but you will soon have an opportunity to mold the future.

FLOWER READING

The late Gordon A. Smith gave me the information for this section of this book. Gordon was a psychic medium, healer and card reader who has been involved with the world of spirituality for many years and he was much respected for his knowledge. Like many of my friends, Gordon has held many posts on the committee of the British Astrological and Psychic Society, including being Chairman on and off over the years.

The method

Flower reading is an unusual form of divination that I hadn't come across until Gordon demonstrated it for me. It requires a good deal of intuition and psychic perception. The Enquirer should choose the flower and bring it to the Reader for interpretation. The flower should be left to rest in a vase or on a piece of tissue until the Reader is ready to begin. The Reader then picks up the flower and reads it from the bottom of the stem up to the top of the bloom. The bottom of the stem represents the Enquirer's childhood while the stem and bloom represent the path of a person's life and his future. The following list shows how to interpret various parts of the flower.

- A roughly torn stem indicates a difficult childhood. A smoothly cut one suggests an easy start to life.
- Smooth sections of stalk indicate smooth periods of life, whereas rough, torn or discolored patches denote times of trouble. Discolored patches suggest marriage or relationship problems.
- New branches bring new beginnings, while a division of the stem denotes choices and different pathways that could be taken.
- Buds that come to nothing suggest losses or situations that don't work out.
- A new shoot or a group of leaves at the appropriate age can indicate the birth of children.
- Strong leaves represent living children, while weak ones that fizzle out denote miscarriages or even losses in infancy.
- Illness may be indicated by a weak patch, such as thinning or twisting of the stalk.
- The bloom shows whether the Enquirer will achieve his current ambitions. A bud represents desires and ideas that have yet to be achieved, whereas an open flower will show success and achievement of goals.

- Friends and relatives are represented by leaves. The Reader must look at the leaves and judge their condition in order to see how these people will affect the Enquirer.
- Career matters that are coming into being will be highlighted by a bud, but when these are in full gear, they will be denoted by a bloom. When they are coming to an end, there will be a bunch of dying petals.
- Anything that is curling up or dying shows that some part of the Enquirer's life is wending its way to a conclusion. Anything that has been attacked by insects is under attack by others or by forces outside the Enquirer's control.
- Thorns symbolize knotty problems.

As you can see, this kind of reading is open to interpretation by the individual Reader, but when added to some psychic ability, it works surprisingly well. Certainly the sample reading that Gordon gave was very successful, and he picked up a number of facts about my past that he could not have known. He also correctly identified a couple of major career decisions that were on my mind at the time of the reading.

He actually told me that an important offer would come to me from overseas when the flower was in full bloom. Over the succeeding days, the bud opened, the flower bloomed and then died. I threw it out with a shrug of my shoulders, but a few days later I received an important offer from Australia—and the letter had been sent on the day when the flower was in full bloom!

THE CRYSTAL BALL

When a client visits a crystal ball Reader, his eyes tell him that there is a solid glass ball with nothing visible inside it, but judging by what the Reader tells him, he assumes that there must be something there! So what is crystal reading? How is it done? Can anyone do it? I put these questions to two friends of mine who use their crystal balls in two completely different ways, and this was the result.

Robin Lown

Robin is a palmist, Tarot Reader, clairvoyant and crystal Reader and he is on the committee of the British Astrological and Psychic Society. This side of his life exists in addition to him having a "proper job" as a school inspector within the British education system. This is what Robin had to tell me about crystal gazing.

Setting the scene

If you want to buy a crystal ball, visit a psychic festival or a shop specializing in these things and have a good look at what is available. Weigh the crystals that you like in your hand and see which ones you feel drawn to, because the shape and size is important. You may even fancy a colored crystal for your readings. Never buy any item of this nature by mail order because you need to try it to see if it feels right. Having said this, most professionals seem to have had their crystals given to them or bought for them, or they seem to acquire their crystal in some odd way.

Before trying to use your crystal, wash it thoroughly in spring water and leave it out in the sun to dry, then meditate on it, asking for it to work for you and also to bring help and guidance to those who consult you. I charged my own crystal by holding it in my hands within my aura and telling the spirit world that I wanted to use it in order to give help, service and truth to those who needed it. I meditated on it as being part of myself, re-affirming myself as a seeker of truth. Even now when I use my crystal, my motives have to be clear. I must want to be of service and help to the Enquirer because any other feelings would disrupt the reading, and I would have to start over again. Most people respect the crystal for what it is and ask permission before picking it up. I have noticed that only crass materialists and those who are totally unaware of spiritual matters attempt to pick it up without asking permission, and I am afraid that I get quite irritated with them when this happens.

How do I read?

I use palmistry first, in order to create a link with the Enquirer, then I give him the crystal to hold. I tell him that it is not necessary for him to think of anything in particular. After this, I ask for the crystal back and I place it on a stand, which is on a piece of black cloth. Then I slowly tune in. I use the crystal as a form of psychometry and I don't think that I actually see anything in the crystal itself. Rather, I see images that are projected from my head in a kind of psychic ventriloquism and a projection of what is in my mind. Firstly, I see scenes, people and situations, and then I begin to feel impressions and emotions. My method is definitely allied to psychometry, clairvoyance, clairaudience and clairsentience.

(I asked Robin whether crystal reading had ever led him to mediumistic experiences where he was in contact with friends or relatives of the Enquirer who had "passed over." He said that this did happen on occasion and that there were also times when he felt himself being "taken over" by someone who wanted to express his or her thoughts through him.)

At this point, I obviously don't know whether the images that I see are of the past, present or future, so I inwardly ask my guiding spirit to tell me. I ask whether this is the past and then wait until I get a yes or no feeling. If the event turns out to be in the past I ask to be shown what relevance this might have to the present—and this often brings another image to me. By now, I will be aware that my chakras** are open and that both the crystal and the Enquirer are within my auric bubble. I then start to tell the Enquirer what I am receiving. As he or she begins to connect with what I am saying, the images and impressions speed up and become more definite, more certain—and then it becomes much easier for me. Sometimes an Enquirer can block me, either because he is skeptical or for some other reason. Then I see or feel only a shaft of light, as though it were coming down a tunnel, at which point I give up and resort to reading the Enquirer's palm or cards, both of which are less subject to psychic disturbance.

I then asked Robin how long he would spend on a reading like this, and he said that it depended upon the rapport that he had with the Enquirer and the amount of information that came through. He told me that he always finished a reading by giving a summary of the main points as he saw them. He also kept a pencil and a pad of paper nearby so that he could sketch an item if he wanted to. He also told me that he tended to see certain particular symbols as his centers were opening up. One of them was the figure of eight symbol for infinity that appears over the Magician's head in the Tarot deck, the other was the caduceus, which is the winged staff carried by the Roman god, Mercury, which signifies enlightenment, healing abilities, and magical powers.

** The chakras are the seven psychic centers in the body that have to open up in order to allow psychic impressions to flow in and out.

Barbara Ellen

Barbara is a full-time professional clairvoyant and medium. She is also a consultant for the British Astrological and Psychic Society. Barbara has had many years of experience; she is highly trained and very skilled and knowledgeable. Although Barbara is not primarily a crystal gazer (she tells me that she finds pure clairvoyance quicker and easier), she can use a crystal ball very well when she is required to do so. This is what Barbara told me.

Preparing a new crystal ball

It is far better to acquire a crystal than to buy a new one—another Reader gave mine to me years ago. Wherever your crystal has come from, the first thing you need to do is to immerse it for twelve hours in salted spring water. Some Readers use a solution of vinegar and water. After this, wash the crystal under running water, ideally from some natural source such as a waterfall or a stream. If you don't have access to a stream, find something that will collect fresh rainwater and then allow the water to flow over the ball. Polish the crystal with chamois leather and leave it in the sunlight for at least four hours. After that, don't ever allow anyone else to touch or even to look into your crystal.

Training and preparation

Some Readers spin the crystal with a finger while they are tuning themselves in, while many others work from mental impressions (as Robin does), but I try to use the crystal itself as it should be used.

Place the crystal on a small plinth that is covered by a black cloth. Ideally the cloth should be silk because it is a completely natural product, although many Readers prefer to use velvet because it has a denser texture. Partially cover or surround the crystal with a second black cloth, which should definitely be made of silk. If you wish, you can darken the room slightly and put on a dim light. Some Readers use a red light as this is known to draw the spirit world close. Practice sessions should always be carried out at the same time of the day and never late at night—this procedure seems to help our spiritual guides to work better. Cup the crystal in the cloth and bring it up so that it is in front of your forehead—that is close, but not touching the "third eye" which is in the center of your forehead. While training you must keep the crystal within your aura. This means keeping it wrapped in its silk or velvet cloths on a table next to you while you sleep, read, and watch television, etc. or in a bag at your side while out and about. Never try to read on a full stomach or if you are upset or angry. Do some yoga breathing each time before you start training or reading. To do this, breath in from the stomach for a count of four, hold the breath for a count of two and let it out on a count of four. Do this exercise four times. Relax, get yourself into a peaceful state of mind and then go ahead.

If you begin to see symbols in the crystal during this time, note them down. You may be aware of certain symbols that are personal to you such as a black cat, a white rabbit and so on. Keep a note of what these mean and build up a vocabulary of signs and symbols.

The crystal should begin to cloud and it is important that when this happens that you remain calm and not let yourself become overexcited or the vision will disappear. Red or orange "smoke" is a warning of danger, blue or green "smoke" is fine. Objects that are colored red or orange are another thing altogether, because only red "smoke" warns you to be on the alert. The visions will go out of focus and then come back sharply into focus, but you will have to wait a few minutes for this to happen—perhaps as long as five minutes. This training period will last for about eight days but you must persevere with it until the ability comes. When an image comes, wait for the message that comes with it. This message will come into your mind through the help of your spiritual guides. Sometimes the objects will come into view first and the clouds later, because every Reader works slightly differently. Be sure to ask your spiritual guides to help you.

When I see images moving in the crystal, I know that those that come in from the left represent events that are coming towards the Enquirer while those on or travelling towards the right are passing away from him. This is how it works for me, but you may see things or do things differently.

As soon as you feel that you are making a link with your crystal, either with mental pictures or actually seeing milky-type smoke or images within the ball itself, find some guinea pigs to sit for you. Try to find people who you know nothing about. Ask your Enquirer to cup his or her hands around the crystal without actually touching it and to remain in that position for approximately two minutes. Then take the crystal back from the Enquirer and relax. Shade the crystal from the light and begin to give out whatever comes. As soon as your sitter can acknowledge that you are getting something meaningful through, it will come through even more quickly. Any kind of feedback will help. Be sure to keep notes so that you can assess your progress and make adjustments in your thinking.

A sample reading

At this point Barbara went on to give me a reading. I hadn't expected this so it was an unaccustomed treat. The first thing that she saw was an airplane. This was not surprising, as I traveled a lot at that time and I was due to take a trip to New York at the time of the reading. She then saw my son Stuart waving a document of some kind. Stuart was about to take an exam in computer and business studies. Barbara also told me that she could see my husband with a pain in his back and leg. This was not surprising as my husband at the time, Tony Fenton, had been doing some heavy work and his back was never strong at the best of times. She then told me that my daughter, Helen, needed new glasses. As it happened, Helen had recently bought some new glasses so that didn't make much sense at the time. But it turned out a few days later that the prescription was wrong and the shop had to make up replacement lenses for her.

FORTUNE TELLING BY DICE

It is a fact that anything that has specific numbers, letters, shapes, colors, denominations or anything else of a regular nature can be used for fortune telling. As long as you assign a particular meaning to each number, letter, shape or color and stick to it, this will work for you. The list below is the way that I would interpret the numbers on the dice, but if you have a favorite system of your own, please feel free to use it.

The method

The simplest method is to use three dice of any size or color. Hold them in your hands for a moment and concentrate on whatever is on your mind—if you wish, you could even blow on the dice. Throw the dice gently onto a table and see what comes up.

If you wish to make things a little more interesting, you can take a pretty piece of card stock and draw a design on it. The design should contain seven areas or segments that the dice can easily fall into. The following suggestions cover the kind of thing that most people are keen to ask about; these are *health, family life, relationships, money, career, property and potluck*. The potluck area can be used for anything that is outside the six basic items.

You can draw a flower with several petals, something that looks Indian or Egyptian, or a series of simple circles or rectangles that are arranged in a group or even within one another—it can be as simple or as artistic as you wish to make it. Then see which segments are activated by the dice and direct your reading accordingly.

The list of meanings

One
A new beginning, the start of something important and a feeling of rebirth. Sometimes this indicates the actual birth of a child.

Two
This indicates a partnership that might be business or personal, and while this will need work and perhaps a little caution, it should be successful. A separation is also possible, or perhaps this is a kind of splitting of resources or of two things that move into two different locations.

Three

This represents a celebration, joy, perhaps a wish that is fulfilled and good news. Sometimes there is sadness, loss or sickness.

Four

This indicates financial and domestic security and putting down roots, also rest and recuperation after a period of hard work or after illness. This should be fine, but sometimes there is a feeling that while much is satisfactory, something more needs to be done.

Five

This is a difficult number that shows trouble and strife, arguments, losses and sickness. Sometimes there is a period of challenge or a time of hard work that works out well. There may be travel in connection with business and sometimes also a little time off to enjoy sports, games and even a little gamble.

Six

This might take you back into a past situation. Alternatively, you may need to abandon the past and look for something completely new. Sometimes this involves travel or relocating, but it can also symbolize a feeling of moving away from trouble and into a more successful environment. There may be a feeling of victory and achievement.

Seven

There will be plenty to do, but you can only cope with this if you break it down into workable segments. Muddles will come to an end and you will soon be able to decide on what to keep and what you wish to abandon. There will be slow growth and development and slow moves forward. Seek out legal or professional advice if necessary.

Eight

This signifies a time when life speeds up. There may be fresh opportunities, a new job, travel and perhaps a new address or environment. There may be something that holds you back, but this seems to be more a case of fear of change or a reluctance to make the effort than a real problem.

Nine

This number suggests happy family life, comfort, a happy home life, satisfaction, safety and money. However, there may also be some kind of worry or heartache due to a family problem.

Ten

Either great success in all things (money, love, health, career etc.) or if other omens are poor there can be a complete collapse of plans or even a stab in the back.

Eleven

This can refer to children, young people or even vague friendships. Otherwise, it relates to news and small events that can lead to larger and more important ones later on. Sometimes this signifies studying, investigating and gathering news—perhaps also the need to keep your ear to the ground.

Twelve

This refers to travel or important visitors from overseas. It can mean a new vehicle or some other new means of transport, a change of address or some other change in your immediate environment. New friendships and possibly a new lover can be indicated.

Thirteen

Women will figure strongly in your life soon, either as friends, lovers, at work, in the family or in any other way. This should be beneficial.

Fourteen

Men will figure strongly in your life soon, either as friends, lovers, at work, in the family or in any other way. This should be beneficial.

Fifteen

This can mean a completely fresh start, but it can also mean an adjustment or improvement in a current situation.

Sixteen

A partnership matter will prove successful. This can be personal or business.

Seventeen

Success in matters connected to love, but business or career matters will be problematic and this may affect your love life.

Eighteen

This suggests that a wish will come true, so it can refer to just about anything that you may be hoping for.

THE I CHING

This is usually pronounced "Eee Ching." This is a Chinese system of divination that dates back in some form to around 8,000 years ago—and it is incredible to consider that this was actually the tail end of the last ice age! The I Ching is known as the "Book of Changes" because the system uses a series of lines that can be read once and then changed for a second reading. There is a method of reading that relies on sticks, and no doubt this predated the invention of coins, but the coin method is the easiest for a westerner to use.

For the reading, you will need a clean table or one with a clean cloth on it, a pen and some paper, plus three coins of the same type. These can be those imitation Chinese coins that you see in Feng Shui shops or ordinary coins, such as a quarter. If the coins are not modern ones, choose which side is heads and which is tails, and then designate the heads as Yang and the tails as Yin. Gather the coins into your hands and focus on a question that is on your mind or on the mind of your questioner if you are doing this for someone else, and then throw the coins down fairly gently.

If two or more coins land with their heads up, draw a complete (Yang) line on your piece of paper but if two or more coins fall with their tails up, draw a broken (Yin) line on your paper. If it happens that all three coins fall with their heads or tails up, mark the line with a small cross, as these will later become your *changing* lines. Do the same thing a second time, drawing your second line above the first, and then repeat the process until you have six lines. This will be your hexagram.

Check the key to the hexagrams on pages 29 and 30 in this book and note down the number of your hexagram. If you have marked any lines with a cross, draw up a second hexagram but change the marked lines from Yang to Yin and vice versa. The second hexagram will offer further information and guidance regarding the question. The following illustration is an example of a hexagram where two lines came about as a result of three heads or tails being thrown. Note the "changes" in the second hexagram.

It is worth noting that the I Ching is far more useful for business, financial and

Hexagram 1	Hexagram 2
———	———
——— ——— X	——— (changed line)
———	———
——— ———	——— ———
——— ——— X	——— ——— (changed line)

practical questions than it is for romantic or family ones. This is because in times gone by, Chinese people married for practical reasons rather than romantic ones, and their main concern was for the family and its survival during hard times. However, with a little imagination, you can adapt the answers to fit any situation. You will also notice that many of the readings stress the importance of modesty and of not throwing one's weight around or being arrogant. It seems that the Chinese believed fervently that arrogance was often followed by a fall from grace.

The I Ching readings in this book are very brief, but if you decide that you would like to know more about the I Ching and other Chinese fortune telling methods, treat yourself to my book, which is called *Secrets of Chinese Divination*.

The I Ching table

Interpreting the Hexagrams

1. Work hard to gain your objectives but don't overreach yourself.
2. To some extent your future happiness is in the hands of others, so don't rush in and grab at it for yourself.
3. Expect to reach your goals in a slow and steady manner. Other people will give you help and guidance.
4. Take advice and expect to learn slowly. Don't put on airs and graces but be ready to listen to the wisdom of others.
5. There is danger ahead, so don't plunge into anything—rather wait until times are better. When you do begin to make a move forward, there will be friends around who will help you.
6. Although you are probably in the right, this is not a good time to argue or to state your point. Accept criticism, even a lack of credit for work that you have done for the time being. Things will soon improve.
7. You will soon have to face some kind of battle, but others will be there to help you. Whether you fight or retreat is for you to decide but you will receive guidance.
8. Peace and harmony surround you now. Be sincere in all that you do and expect to make some efforts on behalf of others as well as for yourself.
9. Times may be hard for a while but with a sensible and economic approach you will achieve your aims, then you will appreciate the good things all the more when they arrive. Restraint, sincerity and regard for others will be needed.
10. Be firm, even with yourself. Tread the straight and narrow road. Don't hesitate or others will take advantage of you and you will lose your stride.
11. Share your happiness and good fortune with others who are less well off. This should be a time to get things done, to plant for the future or to harvest from the past.
12. Move forward slowly and carefully. From small beginnings, you can make

gradual growth but be careful to do this in a modest manner. Doors will soon open for you.

13. There is light at the end of the tunnel. You will soon be able to make better progress and pass from obscurity into a brighter and more successful future. Success will be yours, but you should share the benefits of this with others in order to help them.

14. Work and study will go together. By learning or training, you will be in a better position to understand how to tackle the tasks ahead of you. Don't go overboard in trying to impress others, just grasp the basics and work at the job quietly.

15. Be modest—this will encourage others to help you rather than to stand in your way. Others will admire you for your progress as long as you don't push it down their throats.

16. You will need to advertise both yourself and your wares and to create an enthusiastic atmosphere. Avoid arrogance or self-satisfaction as this will put others off your ideas, and don't fall for your own propaganda.

17. This is a time to drift with the current and to let others show you the way or take the initiative on your behalf. You will be in charge of your own affairs again soon enough.

18. You will soon have to put something right, and you may have to apologize or sort out some kind of misunderstanding. Be scrupulously honest in all your dealings now and be seen to be in the right.

19. In the recent past it was right for you to assert yourself in order to get where you are now, but now is the time to be magnanimous. Be cautious and advance slowly forward. Be generous to others.

20. You will need to keep your eyes open with regard to practical matters, and also to contemplate wider philosophical issues. Don't take things on trust, but be observative and intuitive.

21. Be careful to stress any positive achievements that you have made, however small they may be. Don't allow others to stress the negative or unsuccessful aspects of your life. Don't allow petty jealousy in others to get you down.

22. Dress well and look successful in order to sell an idea to others to give an appearance of success, but once you have accomplished your aim don't continue to live beyond your means. Contemplation and solitude will be necessary to bring equilibrium soon.

23. The odds are against you now. Some aspect of your life will be destroyed so that you can build afresh for the future. Guard against allowing a situation to develop where people who are close to you undermine you from the inside.

24. Attune yourself to nature and to the seasons and develop a sense of timing. A change of seasons will bring improvements and a renewal of energy. Be patient.

25. Don't rush in where angels fear to tread. Be honest and stay within your own limitations. Heaven will guide you. Be unselfish and simple and don't allow temporary setbacks to upset you.

26. You will make great advances in your career but probably not just yet. Work hard and progress slowly, for success is on the way to you.

27. This symbol stands for watchful waiting. This is not a time for accomplishment, so the questioner should take the opportunity to rest and build up his mental and physical strength for future times of action.

28. A heavy branch breaks when it is overloaded; therefore the questioner shouldn't take on too much at this time. It is better to know one's limitations and to work within them.

29. There are pitfalls ahead and any decisions taken now would place you in a worse position than you are presently in. You should wait for better times to come along before taking action.

30. Intellectual pursuits will go well. An intellectual and logical approach to life would be helpful now.

31. Don't envy those who seem to be cleverer or more successful than you are. Remember, the bigger they are, the harder they fall.

32. Stay put, persevere, and allow things to take their course. Haste will bring problems. Don't insist on having things all your own way, because a casual attitude would be far better. Wait, be yourself, and you will get all that you want.

33. There are crafty people around you who will seek to take advantage. Watch out for traps and don't fall into them. However, you will have to use some guile yourself in order to slide out of any tricky situations.

34. If you have to use strong words, back them up with meaningful action or no one will take you seriously and you will be seen as an empty blusterer.

35. Your situation is improving rapidly and your fortunes are on the way up. Be honest in all your dealings and also be open so that jealous people will not be able to point fingers at you later.

36. When depression and hard times arrive, be cautious and restrained, but don't allow yourself to be ground down by misery. Wait: things *will* improve. Just do what you have to do and refrain from moaning to others about your troubles.

37. Attend to your normal daily duties and make your present surroundings comfortable and your present situation happier. Deal with problems right away rather than trying to escape from them. The accent will be on family life where you will have to be fair but also tolerant.

38. Don't insist that you are right, be flexible and allow some leeway to others. Even if you know that you are right, don't ram the fact down the throats of others.

39. If you have a problem, try to go around it rather than to moan about it. Alternatively, you can go out on a limb to solve it. Get help from others and also help others yourself where you can, because one day you may be facing the same problems that they have.

40. An acute situation may come to a head now, after which you will at least know where you stand. Free yourself from unnecessary encumbrances so that you are in a position to move forward confidently.

41. If others help you succeed, don't keep all the rewards to yourself. Redistribute some of the profits so that everyone benefits.

42. Make the most of any opportunity that comes your way but realize that a good deal of your success will be due to luck rather than your own cleverness. It is worth bearing in mind that at times like these, even an incompetent idiot can succeed.

43. Some form of insurance may be necessary now, as even the best placed of people can run into trouble. Don't allow evil to destroy the things that have been good up to now.

44. Don't be influenced by others, especially if they are stronger than you are. Calm persuasion will help you to influence other people both near and far.

45. Opposition will face you soon. Don't tackle this head on or make yourself unpopular by opening your mouth too much. Go with the crowd, or if that is not possible find one good ally and stick to him.

46. Progress slowly and steadily now. Don't give up—just move steadily onwards and upwards.

47. There will be hard times soon. Don't run away from them but look within yourself and find the strength to cope with them. Adversity can sometimes be a good thing as it brings out abilities that you never thought you had. Have confidence, don't beat your head against the wall, stay calm, and cope as well as you can.

48. Work will be monotonous but it has to be done. Share any benefits that you have accrued with others but watch that they don't take the credit for your efforts or place roadblocks in your way.

49. Your outer manner and presentation will improve and you will soon begin to look more impressive to others.

50. Whatever you are doing, take care to ensure that your tools, equipment and vehicles are working properly. Don't worry about small mishaps but guard against major ones.

51. There will be stormy weather ahead. Don't panic, just wait until it passes and then reassess your situation.

52. Take things easily and progress slowly along your present path. Don't try to take any unnecessary gambles or any more difficult jobs than you are already coping with.

53. Develop slowly. Your progress may be imperceptible to others but it exists nonetheless.

54. If you cannot get what you want, want what you can get. If you demand too much you could find yourself overburdened with responsibilities, whereas if you do well in what you are engaged upon right now, you will be appreciated all the more. More opportunities will shortly come your way.

55. You will be inwardly happy and troubles on the outside will not be able to harm you, and they will soon pass away.

56. You may have to travel soon or have to sell yourself in some way to others, perhaps by going out to get a new job. Look to your manner and your appearance and be careful about who you associate with at this time.

57. Be reasonable and others will accept your ideas. Bend with the wind and go along with the majority opinion for the time being.

58. Inner contentment will be reflected outwardly to others and outer harmony will generate inner peace. In other words, a strong spiritual center will be reflected back by others.

59. Don't be inflexible or allow your opinions to harden. On the other hand, don't allow them to dissolve into nothing either. Be reasonable.

60. You will need to be cautious and to accept certain limitations soon. Reserves of energy, goods or money will be needed while you sit out a difficult situation. When doors are once again open to you, you will be able to move through them. In the meantime, go by the rules, even if they are someone else's.

61. Watch out for warning signs: there will be stormy weather ahead.

62. Don't lose your way when storms arrive but make for a safe perch. Don't waste your energy or get upset needlessly.

63. You have gone through considerable troubles to get where you are now, so don't lose all that you have gained through stupid actions. Try not to look backwards too much because your circumstances are changing and you will soon be able to be more optimistic. Work to consolidate what you have achieved so far in order to build for the future.

64. Move forward cautiously, keeping your eyes and ears open. Experience will count for much now. Wait for the right moment to make your move, and then do so with care and caution.

THE RUNES

Seldiy Bate and Nigel Bourne are well known and well respected members of the British psychic and spiritual scene. They can be seen at psychic festivals, they hold workshops on a variety of subjects and they also write for a number of magazines. Seldiy gave me the benefit of her experience as a Rune reader, which helped to bring this chapter to life. Nigel helped us out by adding information, drawing the illustrations and also pouring us all a glass or two of wine.

Ritual and invocation

The best Runes are always those that you make for yourself. It is traditional before beginning this to make a dedication to the Norse god, Odin, who discovered them. Legend tells us that Odin hung himself upside down from the sacred tree, Yggdrasil. He stayed like this for nine days, during which he reached a stage of enlightenment, and then found the Runes among the roots of the tree. Odin is associated with communication, intellect, logic, travel and healing. However, Odin is also particularly associated with divination, and is the head of the Norse gods.

You can begin by burning some incense, which is sacred to Odin, such as mastic gum or tiny strips of hazel wood. Make an invocation to Odin and visualize the god himself while speaking aloud. He has only one eye and hides the empty socket under the brim of a large hat. He also wears a cloak, carries a blackthorn staff and is accompanied by a raven. He rides the magical eight-legged horse, Sleipnir.

The invocation to Odin

Lord of the Northern Wind, by Sea and Sky,
By Baldur's burning Sun and Freya's Moon,
I call upon thee, O Mighty Odin, that I
May learn the secret of each and every Rune!
I have worked the Magicks well and poured
A libation of mead by the trembling blackthorn tree,
Have listened to the Raven's voice and scored
My name upon a hazel wand for thee;
For he that calls the Divine King Odin and proves
Himself to be worthy of the wisdom will hear
The eightfold drumming of Sleipnir's flashing hooves
And know the wisest of the Gods is near.

A gift demands a gift, Grim Guardian of Death
Whisper'd secrets on Odin's sacred breath!

—Seldiy Bate, Summer Solstice, 1987

To make the Runes

Ideally, runes should be made of wood. Hazel wood is traditional, but any type of wood that you like will do (except yew, the tree of Death). If you take a branch from a living tree, don't forget to ask the tree for its permission first. Be careful to select a branch that will not damage the tree irrevocably and place a silver coin somewhere in the tree for payment. Leave the wood a while to season. Slivers of wood can be used or you can cut the branch into slices like a loaf of bread. You will need to make 25 Runes, but it is a good idea to cut more than this number so that you have some to spare if you make a mistake in the lettering.

If you practice magic, cut the letters into the Runes with your own personal magical knife, otherwise cut the letters with any good sharp knife, or burn them in with a pokerwork needle, which you can buy from a craft shop. If you can cope with the idea, you may place a little blood on at least one of the Runes, so prick your thumb with a clean needle. You can mark each Rune with a tiny dot at one end to show which would be upright if you wish to use upright and reversed readings. Darken the engravings on the Runes with red ink (to represent blood), or a mixture of soot and water or maybe some mead, which is sacred to Odin.

Runes can also be made from slivers of bone or soft stone such as limestone. Pebbles of equal size can be used and they look very nice if the design is carefully painted on and then the whole stone is varnished. Any modeling clay that you can buy in a craft shop can be used. This may be the type that you need to fire or the kind that hardens by itself. Failing all this, buy yourself a set of Runes that you feel drawn to. However you come by your Runes, you will need to consecrate them. They should be washed in natural running water (or spring water dripped on the back of each Rune). You should then waft them through some appropriate incense and make a prayer.

Make yourself a bag for your Runes. This can be leather, felt or silk—ideally anything that can be pulled closed with a drawstring. Finally, you should make a Rune wand from a hazel twig or a piece of dowel. This should fit into the Rune bag along with your Runes. You can mark the wand with the Runic symbols for your initials, and then paint, decorate, or varnish it.

Casting the Runes

The simplest method is to ask your Enquirer to dip into the Rune bag and pick out whatever number of Runes you need to work with. Alternatively, lay all

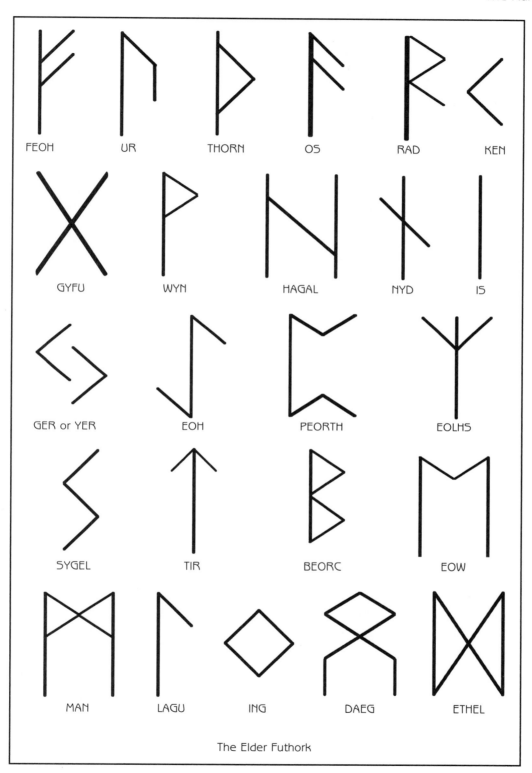

FEOH   UR   THORN   OS   RAD   KEN

GYFU   WYN   HAGAL   NYD   IS

GER or YER   EOH   PEORTH   EOLHS

SYGEL   TIR   BEORC   EOW

MAN   LAGU   ING   DAEG   ETHEL

The Elder Futhork

the Runes out face downwards, ask the Enquirer to swirl them around on the table (or Rune cloth, if used) and then to pick out whatever number you require. He should then hold his chosen Runes in his hands for a few moments while thinking about his life. The Runes can be used for a general reading or to answer a specific question.

Layouts

A clock shape can be used with each Rune representing one month of the year. The clock shape can also represent the astrological houses. Astrology is not a Norse divination but many professional Readers find this convenient because they are familiar with it. Another simple idea is to draw two large circles, the inner one representing the immediate future and the outer one showing more distant events. The inner circle can indicate people and situations that are close to the Enquirer, while the outer one symbolizes the outside environment of work, strangers, and distant situations. A square divided into four could show various areas of life such as the family, work, health and relationships. Indeed, a whole roulette table of sections could be worked out. However, a few basic divisions will help, especially when the Enquirer is a stranger to you, in which case you don't automatically know what is on his mind.

The *Futhork* alphabet and its symbolism

There is some variation in Runic alphabets—this one is sometimes called the Futhork alphabet after its first six letters.

Runic letter : FEOH
English equivalent : F
Key word : Cattle

Cattle represented prosperity or wealth in the ancient world, much as they do in parts of Africa today. So this Rune represents the Enquirer's personal property and funds, his wealth and also status and position. His career (or lack of one), in terms of material security, and sometimes also emotional security. This Rune represents the fulfillment of love, and if appropriate, of pregnancy, as well as fertility and growth of all kinds.

Inverted meaning   Financial loss and a lack of fulfillment. Sexual frustration, difficulties related to procreation. Female health problems, also problems related to weight gain.

Runic letter   : UR
English equivalent : U or W
Key word   : Wild Ox

The wild ox was considered a symbol of great physical strength. It represents masculinity, the active principle and also the physical and material planes. This brings opportunities to better oneself, possibly also a financial improvement, but always with the expenditure of energy or strength. This sometimes denotes the acquisition and controlled use of a physical skill or the training of such in others.

Inverted meaning Missed opportunities. Lack of strength. This may be physical or metaphorical weakness, alternatively perhaps misplaced power or uncontrolled strength.

Runic letter   : THORN
English equivalent : TH
Key word   : A thorn

The thorn protects the plants from predators; therefore this represents protection in all its forms, be they physical, mental or even psychic. This may mean protection from attack, physical defenses, and even the use of an offensive deterrent if other Runes nearby indicate this. This can also mean using verbal defense or protecting others. If there are decisions to be taken, they will require a certain element of caution and self-protection. The Enquirer must allow matters to run their course and not force anything. This Rune can also indicate family matters.

Inverted meaning Making a bad decision. Aggression used for the wrong reasons, perhaps a misplaced use of power, jealousy or an overdefensive attitude. Also, tension and introversion.

Runic letter: OS
English equivalent: A or O
Key word: A god

This Rune is sacred to Odin so can be used in any invocation to him, as Odin is the chief of the gods of magic. This Rune represents authority, superiors, elders and ancestors. Parents and all that can be inherited from them are indicated, as is any kind of father figure or god figure in the Enquirer's life. This can also apply to the Enquirer's spiritual progress, beliefs and philosophy, and it can denote guidance from above.

Inverted meaning   Problems related to parents or authority figures, even government bodies of some kind. An overdominant attitude and abuse of power. Also blind faith, fanaticism, obsession and complexes.

Runic letter: RAD
English equivalent: R
Key word: A wheel

This Rune represents movement; therefore it could suggest a journey with a purpose. This includes transport matters and all kinds of physical movement and exploration but also mental travel, such as studying and using one's imagination. There may be movement in the Enquirer's affairs shortly, especially if there is something that he has neglected or left on the back burner for a while. This Rune relates to changes, the turning of events and progress forward.

Inverted meaning   Difficulties related to travel and transport. Perhaps a journey that is necessary but not enjoyable such as a visit to a sick person or to see someone who is in a position of authority. This may indicate immobility or stubbornness and a lack of imagination or changes for the sake of change that do nothing to enhance the Enquirer's life.

Runic letter: KEN
English equivalent: K or a hard C
Key word: A bonfire

This Rune brings warmth and light into the Enquirer's life and traditionally celebrations—possibly around a bonfire or a barbecue. The Enquirer will be the center of attention and there will be pleasant social gatherings. It can also suggest mental illumination or a burst of creative energy. This Rune is especially lucky for a woman, as she can expect to receive love from a man, whilst a male Enquirer would find himself in the position of giving love. This may indicate the kindling of a new relationship. There is also a feeling of status and success and it may also signify an improvement in health or a period of healing.

Inverted meaning The Enquirer's life may lack warmth and there may also be a lack of direction and guidance—possibly a feeling of blindness. There may be the loss of something that is valuable. There may be health problems, especially heart trouble or a general lowering of resistance.

Runic letter: GYFU
English equivalent: G
Key word: A gift

This Rune may bring a gift, a contract or an opportunity. It suggests that the Enquirer has some kind of useful gift or talent. This also brings beneficial partnerships and happiness in love but it implies that "give and take" must be part of the relationship. In Runic lore, we are never given anything for nothing, so we must be prepared to pay in some way for whatever we receive.

Inverted meaning There may be a loss or even a swindle now. The Enquirer may find that he lacks the necessary talent or qualities for a particular job that he would like to do. This Rune can also suggest a sacrifice, and when inverted it betokens a pointless one such as martyrdom or exploitation. Also an illness or some shortcoming that the Enquirer has to accept.

Runic letter: WYN
English equivalent: W or U
Key word: Joy

This Rune brings joy and happiness on an emotional level. It is associated with water, and therefore it suggests a journey over water or perhaps a home near water. Alternatively, an important visitor could come from over the water. There may be an artistic or spiritual awakening and there may also be gain or luck in respect of creative or inspirational matters. Sometimes this Rune foretells the appearance of a fair-haired man.

Inverted meaning Overemotion, martyrdom and depression. The Enquirer is advised to avoid making major decisions, as he is probably too emotionally involved with the problem at hand. There is difficulty in seeing clearly and also bad judgement. This Rune suggests the need to wait three months before making a decision that is directly related to an emotional matter or three days before making a decision related to work. There may be problems concerning the digestive system or with the body fluids, or in the case of a female with the menstrual cycle or the hormone balance.

Runic letter: HAGAL
English equivalent: H
Key word: Hail

This represents a bolt from the blue that may result from some kind of natural disaster or some unexpected twist of fate. This Rune implies havoc, disruption of plans and unforeseen events. Even good events are possible but they might turn the Enquirer's world upside down. There may be sickness in the family or unexpected pregnancies. The Enquirer must be prepared for the unexpected, but if there is destruction, this allows him to rebuild in a better way. It is even possible that the disaster is self-inflicted or deserved in some way. Sometimes this Rune warns of a death but only if other Runes that are near it emphasize this possibility. It is not worth giving an inverted meaning to Hagal as it means much the same either way up.

Runic letter: NYD
English equivalent: N
Key word: Need

This is associated with necessity, self-preservation and natural, instinctive requirements such as the need for food, shelter and to protect one's children—even perhaps to save one's own skin. This Rune also rules such needs as creativity, the need for a job or a relationship. The motivating force is the need to function and to achieve. There is also a warning here to be patient and to exercise restraint.

Inverted meaning   This seems to imply physical tension and emotional tightness. This may belong to the kind of cautious, greedy, envious personality who is hard to get along with. There is an inability to let go and feelings that are bottled up. This can lead to mental problems, sickness, muscular strain, and all kinds of stress-related factors.

Runic letter: IS
English equivalent: I
Key word: Ice

There is an impediment, an obstacle and a feeling that everything is frozen up. Plans may be halted, money may be immobilized and nothing good can come of the present situation, so the instruction here is to leave things alone and to try again another time. Feelings might be frozen and there may be too much detachment for the Enquirer. This is like the ice of winter that always melts in the spring, so there will be a time of warmth and growth, but patience is needed.

Inverted meaning The same, but worse! There may be fear, coldness and avoidance. There could be some physical impediment such as rheumatism or paralysis. Perhaps there is immobility or mental paralysis with no clear or constructive ideas, in addition to obstinacy and a refusal to adapt.

Runic letter: GER or YER
English equivalent: Y or soft G
Key word: Cycle or harvest

The end of a cycle is in sight and this is like the turning of the seasons or the wheel of fortune. There may be a waiting period, a time of expectation and a promise of fulfillment. The Enquirer will reap what has been sown for good or for ill. This time of change is inevitable and it should be used constructively. This is a time to pay debts, to make a start on new projects, sign contracts and perhaps even to move house. In other words, this is the time for a fresh start.

Inverted meaning This Rune is really much the same either way up but opportunities may be missed as a result of the Enquirer's resistance to change or an inability to see the advantages of a situation. A cycle or a waiting period of a year is indicated.

Runic letter: EOH
English equivalent: E (as in egg)
Key word: Yew bow

The yew bow is flexible enough to adapt itself to a new shape without breaking; therefore this suggests a kind of recoiling, retreating or stepping out of the way of difficulty. The Enquirer will have to take a flexible approach to life and adapt himself to a new and different situation. He may even take one step backward in order to move two steps forwards. Pitfalls will be avoided, and inconvenient situations will turn out advantageous in the end. The Enquirer may be able to use the strength of others against them (as in judo), or to avoid the manipulative behavior of others or their dominance in order to find another way around a problem. He will need to do some lateral thinking.

Inverted meaning There may be indecision, vacillation, and a retrograde step in one's progress. There may be withdrawal, even a relapse into physical or mental sickness. There may be deviousness and craftiness, refusal to face up to problems or escapism.

Runic letter: PEORTH
English equivalent: P
Key word: The secret

Something is not being revealed to the Enquirer and he will only receive the knowledge or information at the right time. If this is the first Rune to appear in a reading, it might be better to leave it and try again a few days or even a few weeks later. This suggests a link with the spirit world, psychism, dreams, visions and trance-like states which may bring forth prophecy. It also suggests unexpectedly good events, luck, abundance, and the return of favors that the Enquirer may have forgotten. Unexpected benefit.

Inverted meaning Imaginary fears, disappointment over an expectation. Favors that are not returned. Lack of communication or going behind someone's back. This Rune can also indicate subconscious fears, phobias and deeply hidden psychoses.

Runic letter: EOLHS
English equivalent: E or Y
Key word: A hand held upright in greeting. A reed

The reed definition of this Rune has connections with the reed in a musical instrument, in that it suggests artistry, poetry and creative talent or self-expression. This denotes hobbies, cultural interests and study for pleasure. The greeting definition signifies belonging to a special group that uses its own behavior and vocabulary.

Inverted meaning   There are people who the Enquirer should avoid, such as a group who behaves in stupid or illegal activities or who are a bad influence. Alternatively, there is a lack of creativity or self-expression or perhaps a lack of opportunity for the Enquirer to express himself in his work or in his life generally.

Runic letter: SYGEL
English equivalent: S
Key word: The sun

The sun was viewed as the source of life in the ancient world and in a way it still is now. Therefore, this Rune represents the life force, health and healing and also rest and recuperation. It rules relaxation and activities such as sport, hobbies, vacations and entertainment. On other levels, it can indicate success, fame, recognition and bringing a creative endeavor or talent out into the light.

Inverted meaning   This is the same as the upright meaning but if the Enquirer has been overdoing things, this tells him that he needs and deserves time off to relax and enjoy himself.

Runic letter: TIR or TYR
English equivalent: T
Key word: Tir, the war god

Tir is the Norse god of war (similar to Mars); therefore this Rune implies activity, energy and heroism. If the Enquirer is male, he will seek romance soon, and if female, there will soon be a new lover or partner. Any ensuing romance would be high-octane, full of passion and overwhelming feelings. There may also be anger, aggression, angst, and attack.

Inverted meaning   Lack of energy or something that is misdirected. For a male Enquirer, a broken love affair or unrequited love, possibly caused by being too pushy. For a female, possibly falling for the wrong person or an obsessive relationship. Other possibilities are sexual frustration, impotence, arguments, damage to property, violence, cuts, burns, bruises, accidents, headaches or allergies.

Runic letter: BEORC
English equivalent: B
Key word: Birch tree

The birch is associated with fertility cults and pagan ritual, particularly that which is concerned with spring and the awakening of the life force. Therefore, this Rune can mean new beginnings, expansion, celebrations, weddings and births. It represents joy in the family but also ritual, familiarity and repetition or routine.

Inverted meaning A plan that doesn't come to fruition, barrenness and delays. It can indicate sickness in the family, disconcerting visits, unfamiliar surroundings, bad news in the community or ill feeling among friends. Also, fatigue and a lack of energy.

Runic letter: EOW
English equivalent: E as in egg
Key word: Horse

This relates to travel and transport, movement and methods of transport such as the Enquirer's car, the bus that he takes, or even his feet. On a working farm, this relates to animals, but it can also signify pets. This Rune is concerned with change, and the methods that are used to bring it about, in addition to ideas and the medium that is used to put them across to others. This is related to all forms of communication and progress, and how they are achieved.

Inverted meaning Problems with transport and delays. Sick animals feature here, as do sick people, immobility and handicaps. Also, failure to get a message across or the wrong approach.

Runic letter: MAN
English equivalent: M
Key word: Man

This Rune represents a male figure, a man in authority or a professional man. The Rune tells the Enquirer not to forge ahead with any project without consulting a professional. This person may be a doctor, lawyer, accountant or perhaps even a plumber, a computer buff or some other form of craftsman, as appropriate. The Enquirer should delay making decisions until after all such consultations have taken place.

Inverted meaning This may indicate problems related to authority figures such as the police, court of law, or the Enquirer's boss. There may be abuse of power or position, or there may be an influential person who stands for something different to the Enquirer. Perhaps there is a domineering father figure around, or maybe a foreigner or someone from an alien environment. If this is a true enemy, look at the surrounding Runes for more information.

Runic letter: LAGU
English equivalent: L
Key word: Lake

This is a feminine Rune that is connected to the moon goddess, the sea, the psychic realms, intuition and the mysteries of childbirth. This symbolizes anything that allows change, fluidity and conduction and any kind of medium. It also applies to protection and a kind of womb-like safety. It can indicate a woman in a reading—although she has to be of an age and type who is capable of giving birth. Thus also fertility and children. This rules the unknown and the universal world of the spirit rather than personal affairs.

Inverted meaning Paranoia and the inability to cope with the subconscious. Blood, menstrual problems or other cyclic problems. Hormone imbalances, miscarriage and infertility. Also escapism, alcoholism, and drug dependence. If the Enquirer is overemotional or too emotionally involved with a problem, he should consult someone impartial.

Runic letter: ING
English equivalent: NG
Key word: The Danes. The family Rune

This represents fertility, production, and material results, also the earth, fruition, and children. The idea is that something produces a result or completes a project, and this can apply to long-term projects or problem solving. It also suggests protection; enclosure, security and staying put in familiar surroundings. If a realistic effort is put into problem solving, at the end of the relevant cycle, they will be solved. This Rune can refer to friends—particularly if they are from overseas. It is also associated with magic, divination and women's mysteries by an association with the mother goddess.

Inverted meaning   There may be a lack of productiveness, a lack of charity or tolerance, and perhaps imprisonment, restriction and tension. This Rune can indicate health problems related to tension, stress, and blockages, claustrophobia and infertility.

Runic letter: ETHEL
English equivalent: E or O
Key word: Inheritance

This denotes benefit through property, gifts, and help from older relatives, also inheritance, heirlooms and an actual object that is left to the Enquirer. It is also associated with documents, wills, legal matters and anything related to money.

Negative or reversed interpretation   The Enquirer may be bound by old conditioning and may refuse to let go of outmoded ideas and concepts. Sometimes this denotes overturning the established order of things and bringing chaos to the family or group. Perhaps the Enquirer needs to consider what benefits you and others.

Runic letter: DAEG
English equivalent: D
Key word: Day

This signifies daytime, warmth and light, so it refers to anything that is open, obvious and easily seen. This represents things that come to light and also face values. It can indicate advertisement, image, clarity and recognition. Also success in studies, passing tests and gaining qualifications, a change for the better and success in general. If this is close to the blank Rune, the success is a matter of fate or destiny. It may be worth setting an appropriate date for something to happen, making relevant preparations and then waiting for it to come around.

Inverted meaning   This Rune means much the same either way up but occasionally it can refer to sunset or the ending of a phase in one's life. It can mean sleep, illness or even coma, also things that are hidden and answers that are not immediately obvious.

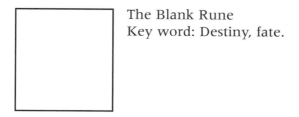

The Blank Rune
Key word: Destiny, fate.

Traditionalists don't use a blank Rune but it has become common for modern Readers to do so. This Rune is associated with fate or anything else that is out of the Enquirer's control. This represents those things that are known only to the gods. Look at the Runes that are nearby to see what the fates have in store or use this in some kind of placement system where the destiny becomes clear by the position of the Rune.

Words of warning

Seldiy and Nigel also supplied the following poem and words of warning.

> *Ye shall find messages and signs to be read*
> *Signs most mighty, signs so strong*
> *Which the soothsayer colored*
> *The high gods made*
>
> *Do ye know how they should be carved?*
> *Do ye know how they should be read?*
> *Do ye know how they should be colored?*
> *Do ye know how they should be tried?*

Seldiy and Nigel tell us that things can go wrong in the following situations. If you ask a frivolous question, you will be given a frivolous answer. If you become bigheaded before you have gained the requisite skills, you will find the skill being taken away from you. Be prepared to study and work hard. By all means practice readings with obliging friends but always accept some payment, no matter how small or in what form. Remember the words of Odin, "A gift demands a gift." Runic lore states that nobody gets anything without some form of payment—even if it is not an obvious one.

DOMINOES

Tradition states that dominoes should only be consulted on rare occasions; for example, no more than once a month, and *never* on a Monday or a Friday. Only three or four dominoes should be selected from the complete set, which should first be stirred around face down on a table. There are several meanings attributed to each domino, so they will need to be applied to the Querent's situation at the time of the reading.

Domino meanings

Double six
This is a very lucky combination that denotes happiness in relationships and luck in a career or in business, and this is also a good omen for anybody who wants a child. Land and property matters are well-starred, while parents will be caring and helpful.

Six/Five
If the Querent is out of work, there will be a new job soon. There is luck in connection with work and relationships but they will need to be worked at. There may be trouble involving children.

Six/Four
Early marriage, with children following soon after. A happy life with reasonable security. The Querent will soon need to be careful regarding legal matters.

Six/Three
Marriage to a reliable person, and stability in relationships. Illness in middle age. A successful journey and good news regarding vehicles.

Six/Two
Love affairs will go well and marriage could be in the air. The partner will be hardworking and sensible with money. If the Querent is involved in any messy business deals, these will go wrong. A useful gift.

Six/One
Two marriages, the second being the happier. Happiness in middle age. Children will travel and do well. A problem is solved.

Six/Blank

News of a death—this may be animal or human. There is a possibility of jealousy and gossip now and accidents are also possible.

Five/Five

Luck, money, a good career and a happy marriage. A house move that is lucky. Also, improvements in health.

Five/Four

Money worries, associated with some kind of partner. Work will bring money and independence.

Five/Three

Luck in money matters. The Querent will never be short of money. Average happiness in relationships. A nice visitor.

Five/Two

Problems in relationships—perhaps unrequited love. A marriage that is made for financial reasons, but which lacks warmth. There could be news of the birth of a child or new enterprises.

Five/One

Parties and social events. A love affair with a charismatic person, but this will not last. Money problems may continue.

Five/Blank

A warning against speculative ventures, also against rushing into marriage. A friend may need the Querent's shoulder to cry on soon.

Four/Four

Parties and social events, sports and the presence of young people. Manual work will go well but professional people will experience difficulties.

Four/Three

Disappointments, especially concerning children. Illness is possible, as are problems in connection with a vehicle.

Four/Two

Family and domestic upheavals. Unexpected events concerning the home—these could be good or bad. Beware of flirtations or philandering types of people.

Four/One

A good marriage with comfort and security, but possibly without children. The Querent will have to pay some outstanding bills soon.

Four/Blank

There will be trouble in connection with relationships, and any reconciliation will only be temporary. There is a possibility of twins coming into the family. A new outlook or a different way of life.

Three/Three

Money will come to the Querent soon, possibly via a legacy, a win or a bonus. The Querent's love life may go through a bad patch due to outside interference.

Three/Two

This is a good omen for the start of an enterprise. A journey will be enjoyable and worthwhile. Dishonesty will be found out and the Querent should not take any chances now.

Three/One

A surprise and good news. The Querent may become involved in an affair that lands him in trouble.

Three/Blank

Jealousy, broken friendships. Domestic problems due to the weak attitude of the partner or of other family members.

Two/Two

All partnerships and relationships will go well, but health needs to be watched.

Two/One

Loss or failure in business, and if the Querent isn't careful, he could lose his home as well. A flamboyant but unsettled love life.

Two/Blank

Journeys will have a good outcome. Sales and communication ventures will go well. The Querent must beware of thieves. Relationship matters are not good just now.

One/One

Love, money and luck, also happy family life. Parents will be helpful. A decision will be needed soon, but this will require courage.

One/Blank

A visitor comes from over water. Money or resources are in danger of being wasted. Health improves.

Blank/Blank

Loss, theft, disappointment. Troubles are on the way and this could affect the Querent's job, relationships, health or all three. The Querent should also try to guard against accidents.

PLAYING CARDS

Playing cards are a relatively recent invention that first came into being in France in the 17th century. They are a spin-off from the Minor Arcana of the Tarot deck and also from chess, which itself is a spin-off from the Tarot. A playing card deck comprises fifty-two cards that are arranged in four suits. These suits are similar to those found in the Tarot, but with the Jack replacing both the Page and Knight and the Joker standing in for the Fool in the Tarot, and indeed for all twenty-two cards of the Major Arcana. The huge popularity of the Tarot is a relatively recent phenomenon because up to the 1970s most skilled card Readers used playing cards.

Playing card links

The four suits in a deck of playing card suits can be linked to those of the Tarot and also to the four elements.

Playing card	Tarot card	Element
Clubs	Wands	Fire
Diamonds	Coins	Earth
Spades	Swords	Air
Hearts	Cups	Water

A new deck

Buy yourself a new deck of cards, keep them in a box away from other people and use them solely for fortune telling. If you care to make a prayer over the cards before using them for the first time, please do so. It is a good idea to bless the cards and to ask for guidance so that you use them well. Ask for them to bring comfort, help and good advice to your Questioners. If you like incense you can use a joss stick while performing this blessing ritual. Shuffle the cards thoroughly several times to remove their newness and to help them tune into your aura and vibrations.

Spreads

There are many layouts that can be used, including any that you find in a book on the Tarot or even the Runes. If you wish, you can use the cards in conjunction with the twelve astrological houses or the Sephirot of the Kabbala. A Romany fortune teller named Sally showed me the following spread:

Ask your Questioner to shuffle the cards and then spread them out in a rough line face down on the table. Ask him to select fifteen cards and to place them in a rough arrangement face up on the table. Ask him to spread them out a little, keeping them in the same rough area so that you can see which cards touch each other or which are close to each other. The cards that are close to each other link together in some way. After giving the initial reading, go through the whole process again using twenty-one cards and see what develops from the first reading. It is always interesting to note which cards turn up in both spreads.

If you need to time a future event, you can ask your Questioner to select twelve cards and then read each for one week ahead. These can be laid out in a circle. Other spreads might be a horseshoe, a cross or three lines of three cards, with one line representing the past, the second indicating the present and the final showing the past. Frankly, any spread that makes you happy is fine.

In my experience playing cards are always read in the upright position, but tradition assigns several of the cards a reversed meaning. If you wish to use these meanings, you will need to mark the cards so that you know when they are reversed.

Some card Readers only use thirty-two cards, omitting the lower numbered cards altogether but the following list includes all fifty-two cards. There are many different forms of interpretations in use but the following list is probably familiar to card Readers. If you discover other interpretations that suit you better, please feel free to use them.

Ace of Hearts
Joy, love, friendship or the start of a romance.
Reversed
Friendship rather than romance, possibly the end of a love affair.

King of Hearts
Traditionally this represents a fair-haired man who is kind, loving and affectionate and who will give the Questioner good advice.
Reversed
Poor judgment. An unreliable philanderer.

Queen of Hearts
Traditionally this signifies a fair-haired woman who is kind, loving, and good to the Questioner. She is faithful and affectionate.
Reversed
An over-materialistic attitude. A pleasant, but lazy and greedy woman.

Jack of Hearts

Traditionally speaking, this is a fair-haired young man. Look around at the nearby cards to judge his intentions.

Ten of Hearts

Good luck, love and joy. This card improves any bad cards around it and it confirms the benefits of any good ones.

Nine of Hearts

This is called the "wish card" and it confers health, wealth, status and esteem. It signifies an improvement in all circumstances.

Eight of Hearts

Visits and visitors, journeys for pleasure and meals in good company.
Reversed
Irritating visits or visitors.

Seven of Hearts

An unfaithful or unreliable person. Disturbing news.

Six of Hearts

A generous person, and perhaps a shoulder to cry upon. Shared confidences, unexpected propositions and good luck.
Reversed
A friend needs the Questioner's help.

Five of Hearts

Money coming, but also jealous or unreliable people around.

Four of Hearts

A journey or a change. If applicable, the Questioner will marry later in life.
Reversed
An irritating journey or an unexpectedly awkward change in circumstances.

Three of Hearts

The Questioner needs to exercise caution. Rash statements will upset others.

Two of Hearts

Success, happiness, luck and prosperity. An engagement or even a marriage.

Reversed
The same but delayed.

Ace of Diamonds

An engagement or wedding ring. A letter bringing good news about money.
Reversed
Similar but delayed.

King of Diamonds

Traditionally speaking, this is a fair or gray-haired man who is obstinate or powerful but also helpful to the Questioner.
Reversed
An angry, obstinate man, who will hurt the Questioner, or look for revenge for real or imagined slights.

Queen of Diamonds

Tradition suggests that this is a fair or gray-haired woman who is flirtatious, sophisticated and fond of socializing.
Reversed
A very nasty piece of work.

Jack of Diamonds

This is traditionally said to be a fair-haired relative. This person is selfish, dishonest and only interested in his own requirements and opinions.
Reversed
Avoid this person at all costs.

Ten of Diamonds

Money, journeys, possibly help from a married man who lives in the countryside.
Reversed
Similar but delayed.

Nine of Diamonds

A surprise regarding money. This is good if the card is upright but poor if it is reversed.

Eight of Diamonds

A marriage late in life, but this is not necessarily good. Plans and ideas.
Reversed
A bad late marriage.

Seven of Diamonds

A gift or surprise.

Reversed

Waste, the loss of something valuable.

Six of Diamonds

Problems in a marriage, especially if this is a second marriage.

Reversed

The Questioner shouldn't even contemplate a second marriage.

Five of Diamonds

Success in business or other enterprises. If applicable, good children.

Reversed

Success, but this is delayed.

Four of Diamonds

Inheritance or improvement in finances.

Reversed

Annoyances and irritations.

Three of Diamonds

Legal problems, especially if the Questioner is involved in a divorce. A bad marriage partner who will make the Questioner unhappy.

Reversed

Divorce; domestic, and legal problems.

Two of Diamonds

A love affair that meets with opposition.

Reversed

A disappointing love affair.

Ace of Clubs

Wealth, success and peace of mind, also a happy home life.

Reversed

The same, but milder.

King of Clubs

Traditionally, a dark-haired man. He is honest, helpful, humane and affectionate. A faithful partner who makes everyone around him happy.

Reversed

This man may be troubled, in a difficult situation or just plain tricky and dishonest.

Queen of Clubs

Tradition says that this is a dark-hared woman who is businesslike, capable and very attractive to the opposite sex.

Reversed

This woman may be worried or not in a position to help the Questioner. Alternatively, she may be calculating and shifty.

Jack of Clubs

Traditionally this is a dark-haired young man who is a reliable and helpful friend.

Reversed

This young man is either unwilling or unable to help the Questioner right now.

Ten of Clubs

Money is coming. This might be a bonus, a win, a legacy, a raise, or a business idea that takes off quickly.

Reversed

The same, but milder and slower to materialize.

Nine of Clubs

Achievements—and if applicable, a new lover.

Reversed

Obstacles and disagreements.

Eight of Clubs

A greedy, jealous person who is very fond of money comes into the Questioner's life.

Reversed

Opposition, arguments.

Seven of Clubs

Happiness, joy and prosperity. However, the Questioner should be careful in dealings with the opposite sex, as they will cause trouble.

Reversed

The same, but milder.

Six of Clubs

Business success, especially in partnerships.

Reversed

The same, but milder.

Five of Clubs

An advantageous marriage and helpful friends.
Reversed
Friendship rather than marriage.

Four of Clubs

Changes for the worse, lies, and betrayal.
Reversed
Unreliable people around the Questioner.

Three of Clubs

Marriage to a wealthy partner.
Reversed
Marriage to a reasonably comfortable (but not rich) partner.

Two of Clubs

Disappointments, disagreements.

Ace of Spades

Love affairs, passion and obsession. Perhaps also deceitful friends.
Reversed
A death around the Questioner.

King of Spades

The tradition says that this is either a very dark or very fair-haired man who is ambitious. He is a terrific friend but he must guard against losing all that he has.
Reversed
An ambitious, tough, selfish and aggressive man.

Queen of Spades

Traditionally a very dark or very fair-haired woman. Tradition suggests that she is a widow or divorcée. She can be seductive and unscrupulous.
Reversed
A spiteful, jealous woman.

Jack of Spades

This is traditionally a very fair or very dark-haired young man. He is a well-meaning man who never really gets his act together.
Reversed
A lazy, shiftless man.

Ten of Spades
Worry, imprisonment of any kind. This will cast a cloud over any cards that are nearby.
Reversed
The same, but milder.

Nine of Spades
Domestic worries, possibly the total loss of money. Calamity, deaths, natural disasters, destruction, and war.
Reversed
Still terrible, but not quite as devastating.

Eight of Spades
Opposition from others, canceled plans and obstacles.
Reversed
Bad news, opposition and troubles.

Seven of Spades
Sorrow, warnings, losses, and possibly the death of a friend.
Reversed
Still bad, but milder. Expect tears and sleepless nights.

Six of Spades
Improvements, wage increases and rewards.
Reversed
No real recognition for work that is done.

Five of Spades
Good marriage and domestic happiness, but bad-tempered people around the Questioner, albeit outside his home environment.
Reversed
Interference from others, anxiety.

Four of Spades
Illness, business, and money worries.

Three of Spades
A marriage to a wealthy partner who is fickle and unreliable.
Reversed
Possibly a hasty decision. A journey and a parting.

Two of Spades
Scandal, gossip, betrayal.
Reversed
A possible death around the Questioner, or loss and partings due to interference by others.

Combinations

Playing cards can be read singly or in combination with other cards and there are two approaches to this. The simplest and most effective way is to look at groups of cards that fall close to each other and see if they link together to tell some kind of story. There is another method that I have seen described in French fortune telling books and that is to group cards together in a way that creates a specific meaning. There are far too many of these for a beginner to remember, but the chart on page 63 is a list of some basic groupings that are not too hard to cope with.

Basic Combinations

	Four Cards	**Three Cards**	**Two Cards**
Aces	Great success and a completely new way of life. The career is especially positive.	Success and help to the Questioner. Good news and luck.	Partnership, possibly a marriage. Unusual news.
Kings	Great success, advancement, inheritance.	Success. Important business meetings that will benefit the Questioner.	Some success, good business partnerships.
Queens	Scandal but also social activity.	Backbiting and nasty remarks coming to the Questioner. Also invitations.	Some minor gossip. Also an interesting meeting with a female friend.
Jacks	Quarrels. Also noisy parties.	Some quarreling.	Argument and discussion. Someone has bad intentions towards the Questioner.
Tens	Change for the better all round.	Money, improvement of circumstances and finances.	Money, a debt repaid.
Nines	Good luck, unexpectedly good events.	Success, most things will go well. Good health, happiness.	Reasonable success. Important documents to deal with.
Eights	Problems, troubles, worry. Short trips to see friends.	Family problems, love troubles. It is best to postpone decisions until better times come along.	Worry. A desire for love but disappointment as this will not come along yet.
Sevens	Several enemies. Disputes, scandal, conspiracies.	Some people seem to be against the Questioner now. Illness.	One active enemy, but the Questioner will overcome problems, reach success, and make achievements.

PHRENOLOGY

Phrenology, the study of reading the bumps on a person's head, seems like a truly silly idea—but it works! One cannot read the future by this method, but it is a way of reading a person's character. After all, if the lines on a person's hands and feet and marks on the eyes can tell a story, why not the bumps on his head? To some extent, this particular divination has been consigned to a kind of "museum" of divinatory skills, but there is some information available about it on the Internet.

Dr Franz Joseph Gall, a native of Baden, Germany, postulated that there is a connection between the way the mind works and the shape of the cranium, so it was he who developed the concept of phrenology. His idea was that the shape of the head indicates the kind of mind that is contained inside it. He also suggested that a young person's brain could be altered by education and specific kinds of use. This latter statement has proved to be true—and not only for young people, as it is now understood that elderly people's brains remain functioning if they continue to use them. Unfortunately, phrenology was hijacked by the Nazis, as a way of showing who was or was not truly "Aryan" and therefore fit to live in Hitler's third Reich.

The seven major divisions of the head

The Victorian phrenologists started by measuring the head to see if it fitted their concept of normality. Any hat maker will tell you that the shape and size of heads vary enormously among perfectly normal people. Phrenologists then went on to divide the head into seven spheres, which like so many divinations, they linked to the Sun, Moon, and those planets that were visible with the naked eye.

A. Associated with the planet Mercury, this is considered to be the seat of the main intellect and the ability to think. This also governs practical things like being able to judge size, distance, people, places, rhythms and so on.
B. Associated with the planet Jupiter, this concerns the things that we find ourselves naturally drawn to, and it rules anything that captures our loyalty and devotion. It seems to affect those things that we are able to appreciate.
C. Associated with the planet Saturn, this is concerned with our survival instincts. It rules our urge to protect and safeguard others and ourselves. This seems to rule behavior.

The seven major divisions of the head

D. Associated with the Sun, this governs the whole workings of the mind. It is concerned with our ambitions and the way we set about achieving them. This is concerned with status.

E. Associated with the planet Mars, this is concerned with our energies, natural instincts and appetites. It rules such things as our willingness to fight for what we want and the acquisition of material possessions. This also seems to rule the way that we go about things.

F. Associated with the planet Venus, this concerns feelings, affection, love and sex. This is clearly about personal relationships.

G. Associated with the Moon, this concerns our relationship with our family, our home situation and our place in society. This rules the relationship with the home and family.

The forty-two areas of the head

The seven sections have been subdivided into a total of forty-two sections as per the diagram below. I have retained the rather archaic titles of the areas as they were in 19th-century texts, but I have modernized the descriptions to make them clear to today's readers.

The 42 sections of the head

Area A

1. *Individuality*. The power of observation and the ability to discriminate. The larger the bump, the more a person likes dealing with details. If the bump is too large, he will be ultra-critical and very inquisitive; if too small, he will have little curiosity and poor mental faculties.

2. *Eventuality*. A large bump denotes a good memory, while a small one suggests a poor memory and a low level of intellect.

3. *Comparison*. Reasoning ability and powers of analysis. If over-large, this person will be hypercritical; if too small, he will not be able to make comparisons or apply himself to anything.

4. *Causality*. This word, so beloved of psychologists has probably changed its meaning since the 19th century, but in those days it referred to powers of deduction. If this area is large, it means that the person has an original mind, good powers of deduction and intuition. It suggests that he would make a good explorer or inventor. If it is small, the mind will be mundane and shallow.

5. *Mirthfulness*. The sense of humor. Obviously a small bump here would suggest that the subject couldn't readily see a joke.

6. *Locality*. A sense of direction and a memory for places. If large the subject would have a photographic memory and perhaps also occasional flashes of déjà vu. If small, this suggests that the subject finds visualization difficult and that he lacks a sense of direction.

7. *Time*. A sense of rhythm and timing, also punctuality. A small bump here indicates a lack of rhythm and a tendency to be late for everything.

8. *Tune*. If this bump is developed, the subject has an ear for music.

9. *Calculation*. A large bump here indicates an aptitude for figures.

10. *Order*. If this bump is large, the subject is well organized and able to work systematically. If it is small, he will be unorganized and a messy thinker.

11. *Color*. The ability to judge shades of color and to remember them, and the ability to distinguish distant objects. If the bump is large, the subject will be able to use color exceptionally creatively; if small, he may have difficulty in seeing objects at a distance and he may be colorblind.

12. *Weight*. This governs the ability to judge the weight of objects, the ability to balance objects on top of each other or in keeping one's own balance.

13. *Size*. This governs the ability to judge the size of an object or the space of a room.

14. *Form*. This relates to the ability to see and remember people and objects. Artistic people have a well-developed bump here. An over-large bump can make the subject oversensitive to atmospheres or places, while a small one indicates a person who is oblivious to people and to his surroundings.

15. *Language*. A well-developed bump belongs to a good communicator who has a way with words and it can indicate an aptitude for foreign languages. If over-large the subject will talk too much, while if small he will be reticent, hesitant or fumbling in his speech.

Area B

16. *Humanity*. Sometimes called the bump of intuition, this gives deep understanding of the motives of others. If underdeveloped, the subject cannot understand others and is indifferent to them.

17. *Benevolence*. If this area is overdeveloped, the subject will be over-generous towards others; if underdeveloped, he is miserly with his time and his money.

18. *Veneration*. A respect for values and traditions. If the bump is overdeveloped, this might indicate a religious fanatic; if small he will hold nothing sacred and he might have a destructive nature.

19. *Agreeableness*. Popularity, charm and pleasantness. If the bump is over-large, the subject could be effusive or too keen to make himself liked while if small, he is hostile and offensive.

20. *Imitativeness*. The ability to learn through imitation. A small bump here might suggest an independent and eccentric manner or a lack of ability to learn by imitation.

21. *Spirituality*. Religious or spiritual feelings. If the bump is over-large, the person will be too otherworldly to cope with daily life. If it's small, the mind will only be able to cope with things that can be seen, touched heard, etc.

22. *Hopefulness*. Optimism and forward thinking. Too large a bump denotes a lack of realism, while a very small one represents a pessimist.

23. *Ideality*. An appreciation of beauty and the better things for which man strives. If the bump is over-large, the subject is unrealistic; if small, he will lack imagination, culture or ideals.

24. *Sublimity*. A love of romance as in romantic scenery, thrilling experiences, the wild grandeur of places and appreciation of all that is best in the world. If the bump is over-large, the subject will over-dramatize everything; if small he will have no romance in his soul and he will be a wet blanket.

Area C

25. *Firmness*. This bump endows the subject with determination and self-discipline but if it is over-large he will be a tyrant or a despot. If it's small, the person will be irresponsible and unable to finish anything that he starts. He may be easily led into temptation and easily bullied by stronger people.

26. *Conscientiousness*. If this is over-developed the person will be nervous and neurotic; if small he will be indifferent to the needs of others and he will lack principle.

27. *Caution*. If the bump is over-large the subject will be too fearful to achieve anything; if small he will be reckless.

28. *Secretiveness*. A bump here denotes the ability to keep a confidence. An over-large bump denotes a crafty person who enjoys plotting against others, while a small one belongs to someone who cannot keep quiet about anything.

Area D

29. *Self-esteem*. This could be the most important area of all, because without self-esteem we can achieve nothing and we lay ourselves open to manipulation by stronger or less principled people. If the bump is very large, the person will be pompous and full of self-aggrandizement; if small he will be self-effacing and easily pushed around.

30. *Approbativeness*. This area concerns status and standing in the community and the amount of praise that we attract. It rules politeness and social skills. If the bump is large the subject may be full of himself. Alternatively, he may be famous, respected or an authority on a particular subject. If small, he will be indifferent to the opinions of others and perhaps also antisocial.

31. *Continuity*. Concentration and mental application. If the bump is over-large, the subject could be obsessive, but if it is small, he won't be able to concentrate on anything for long.

Area E

32. *Constructiveness*. This is the bump of the maker and doer, the do-it-yourself expert or the creative dressmaker, cook or artist. A large bump here could indicate a person who is always busily engaged with one project or another. A small one denotes a lack of dexterity and a lack of interest in making anything.

33. *Acquisitiveness*. The ability to earn money, to collect goods and also to obtain knowledge. Obviously, if this is over-large, the subject will be a miser and hoarder, and he may lack honesty due to an intense desire to amass things. A small bump denotes a drifter or perhaps someone whose values are not materialistic.

34. *Alimentiveness*. This bump is concerned with the connection between the brain, the sense of taste and the stomach. It regulates the desire to eat and drink. If it is over-large, the subject will be a glutton and a drunkard. If it is very small, he will not be interested in eating and drinking. To quote an ancient book, "fakirs and other hermits who considered starvation to be necessary to their spiritual well-being have very small bumps of alimentiveness." This seems to indicate that eating and drinking is less due to mind over matter than to one's nature!

35. *Execution*. This area could be termed executive talent, as it concerns the ability to create and run some kind of enterprise. There is a kind of destructive or revolutionary aspect to this bump, which suggests that if it is over-large, the subject will seek to break down the existing status quo and impose one of his own making. A small bump here signifies an inefficient and ineffective type of person who wants peace at any price.

36. *Combativeness*. This area concerns resistance, courage, and the ability to stand up for oneself. If the bump is over-large, the subject will be aggressive; if very small he will be a coward.

37. *Vitativeness*. The area reveals the will to live life to the fullest. With a very large bump, the subject will struggle for survival against any odds. If it is very small, he may have little tenacity and no great desire to live. A lack of a bump here could indicate suicidal tendencies.

Area F

38. *Friendship*. This bump indicates the ability to be sociable and to make friends. If the bump is over-large, the subject will be indiscriminate and over-friendly. If small, he will be unfriendly.

39. *Conjugality*. This area rules the ability to make lasting relationships or to make a success of marriage. A normal or large bump here belongs to a relater, while a small one denotes a loner. If the Amativeness (No 40) bump is large and the Conjugality bump small, the subject will want love and sex without having to work at a steady relationship.

40. *Amativeness*. This rules the sexual instincts. If large, the subject will be a sensualist—and over-large bump here denotes someone who prizes sexual conquests over other forms of relationship. If small, the subject will lack sensuality or sexual desire.

Area G

41. *Inhabitiveness*. This area indicates a love of home life and also a love of one's country. If over-developed, this subject could hang on to his home at any cost, or he (or she) could make a great fuss of the home and its contents. If the bump is small, the subject may be something of a drifter with little regard for a home or even for his country.

42. *Philoprogenitiveness*. This area governs a love of and desire for children—also a love of pets. If the bump is very large, this person might relate better to children and pets than to adults. If small, he will not be interested in either children or pets.

FACE READING

These days we see face reading as a Chinese art—and so it is, but there is some evidence that a form of face reading was also known in Europe in the 19th century. This chapter gives a little information on both the Chinese and European systems. Unlike the previous chapter on phrenology, face reading can indicate the kind of fortune a person can expect as well as giving some indication as to his character.

To some extent, we all read faces all the time. When we look at someone who is new to us, we unconsciously assess him and form our opinions about him. In addition to this instinctive form of face reading, there exist far more detailed methods of incorporating rules that have been carefully worked out over a long period of time. The best exponents of this skill are undoubtedly the Chinese. In common with all other serious forms of divination, this is a deep and difficult subject to master, but in this book I shall just dip into the subject in order to give you a brief introduction to a fascinating skill.

Chinese face reading

The Chinese call the forehead area down to the eyebrows *heaven*, and this is associated with the early years of life. The middle area is called *human*, and this is associated with the middle years. The lower section, from the base of the nose down to the bottom of the face is termed *earth*, and this is concerned with old age.

Any part of the face that is scarred, malformed, dented or discolored suggests a problem with the aspect of the subject's life that is associated with that segment of his face. Grey or black marks, whether they are permanent or temporary, denote problems that are themselves either permanent or temporary depending upon the type of mark. Even if the discoloration is caused by a trick of the light, it will mean something. In every form of divination, intuition plays its part, so if yours kicks in while trying out this or any other divination, allow it to flow through.

Heaven
Positive: If this area is clean, clear, and well developed, the subject will have a good start in life with wonderful parents and a useful education.
Negative: Scarring, dents or discoloration here indicate a troubled childhood and a poor education. The problems will be worse for a man if the disfigurement is on the left, and for a woman if it is on the right. A wide forehead is

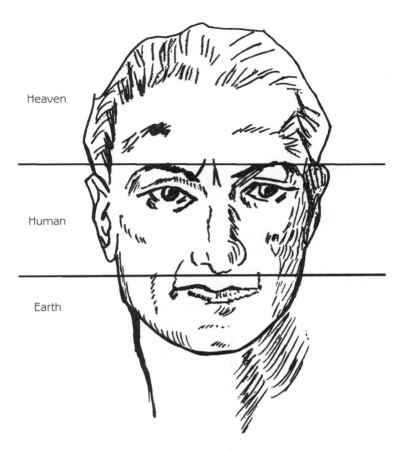

The three major areas of the face

generally considered to be beneficial—but in a woman, a very wide forehead suggests poor personal relationships. The lines on the forehead can be lucky or unfortunate, depending upon where they are situated.

Human

Positive: The middle section of the subject's life will be happy and productive, with stability in relationships and success in the career.

Negative: The opposite of the positive reading. A human section that is longer than either of the other two represents a determined and self-disciplined personality.

Earth

Positive: A happy old age with good relationships with children and grandchildren. Prosperity in life and a comfortable old age.

Negative: The opposite of the positive reading.

The 13 divisions of the face

The thirteen divisions of the face

The Chinese further divide the face into thirteen subsections. Here is a very simplified version of the thirteen-section reading, starting from the top of the face and working downwards.

1. If this is clean and clear, the subject will have a happy childhood and youth, and a good relationship with his parents. His parents should live to a ripe old age. If it is marked or misshapen, there will be unhappiness during youth due to poverty or discord within the childhood home. Veins, dark marks and so forth here signify accidents and sudden losses of money and prestige. A widow's peak suggests that the father will die before the mother.

2. This is similar to the above, but it reveals more about the mother than the father. Negatively, a marked area suggests that the subject will not be believed when he is telling the truth.

3. A good complexion here indicates a fortunate and successful life, whereas discoloration tells of a bad period in the subject's career.

4. If this is dented, the intellect will be low. If scarred, bumpy or sporting a mole, the subject will be impatient and largely unable to bring his plans to fruition as a result of bad public relations skills or bad luck. He will also find it hard to make and keep friends.

5. If this area is healthy, the subject will receive an inheritance and he will succeed in business. Eyebrows that meet or almost meet denote failure, bad luck and a lack of respect from other people. Marks, scars and black moles can indicate anything from adoption to sickness and failure—even a term of imprisonment! Wrinkles or creases between the eyebrows are considered to be all right if the subject is over forty years old, otherwise they denote difficulties, tension and possibly a jealous nature.

6. Grayness here denotes sickness; whereas a green tone indicates adultery. A mole suggests stomach problems, emigration or even imprisonment!

7. Moles here suggest stomach trouble, relationship problems or possibly a partner who is sick. Darkness here tells of a sickly child.

8. A high bony nose suggests failure in business. Moles and discoloration signifies a sick husband and difficulties with females.

9. The tip of the nose should be full in shape and clear of marks, hairs and blackheads for good fortune.

10. This is the groove between the base of the nose and the mouth. If the base of the groove is wider than the upper part and the indentation is neither too deep nor too flat, the subject will have healthy children and he will achieve a high level of wealth and status in life. If it is wider at the top and shallow in shape, the subject will experience difficulties in having children, and his nature may be sour and ill mannered. Relationships will be difficult. If the area is bent, the subject will be childless and he will also be deceitful and unpopular. A straight line that is marked down the middle of the groove denotes children late in life.

11. The mouth. This should be reasonably full with a pinkish color and upturned corners to ensure prosperity, good health and a happy marriage.

12. If this area is dark in the morning, the subject should avoid traveling across water during the course of that day. A man who has a hairless gap beneath his lower lip or a person of either sex who has a scar or discoloration in this area must be careful of their diet, as their stomach may be weak.

13. This should be round, slightly protuberant and strong in appearance. A sharp chin is unlucky. If the chin points to the side, the subject will hold grudges against others. Any scarring or discoloration denotes money losses, possibly the loss of an inheritance. This can also foretell family sickness and accidents.

English face reading

Face shapes

Oval-shaped face

1. *Round or oval*: A pleasant, friendly person who needs a good home and family life. Good judgement and intuitive faculties and a desire for justice and fair play. This person can work hard and is capable and efficient, but he can also relax when necessary. A well-balanced personality.

Square-shaped face

2. *Square or rectangular*: Dynamic, determined and capable. This person has leadership qualities and physical strength. Strong-willed, opinionated, intelligent, and tough. Dexterous, mechanically minded, and active, this subject would make a good soldier.

Triangular-shaped face

3. *Triangular or heart shaped* sensitive, creative, intellectual and with a good mind and memory. Can be hard to understand due to moodiness. A dreamer who needs direction in life. Restless and easily bored.
4. *Round/triangular*: Intellectual and businesslike but also restless and moody. Over-optimistic and over-confident at times. Finds honest self-assessment difficult.
5. *Round/square*: Active, cheerful, opinionated and egotistical but also capable and businesslike.
6. *Square/triangular*: Clever, impetuous, inventive, active. Prospers as a result of creativity.

Side view profiles

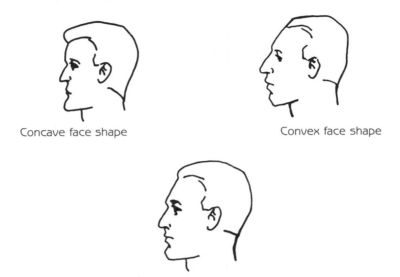

Concave face shape

Convex face shape

Straight face shape

Concave: Steady, rather inflexible. Appears deep and clever but may not be so. Wastes time fiddling about with minor matters. Reserved, interested in the past, good memory.

Convex: Lively, clever, quick thinking. A talker and doer rather than a listener. Practical, quick-on-the-uptake, active. Soon becomes bored and restless, so needs variety in his daily life and in his job.

Straight: Calm, deliberate, reasonable and patient but stubborn, tenacious and strongly opinioned. Has the patience to work things out thoroughly. (I have noticed over the years that many actors on film and television have a straight profile, which confirms that they have the patience to learn lines and put up with the utter boredom of filming.)

The forehead

If this is well proportioned and free of marks, scars, and discoloration, the subject will have a good start in life and a good relationship with his parents. Otherwise, a large forehead denotes a deep thinker, while a narrow forehead denotes an analytical thinker. A forehead that is flat or dented inward suggests good concentration and a cautious temperament, while one that bulges outwards suggests shrewdness and good powers of observation. A low forehead is supposed to indicate a nature that is practical rather than intellectual.

The eyebrows

Clean, clear, and gently curving brows indicate refinement, humor, intelligence, and a lucky life. Curved eyebrows suggest an inquiring mind and arched ones or those that flip up and then down at the ends indicate a creative imagination. Bushy ones belong to more temperamental types, who can be unpleasant at times, while very thin ones denote a fussy nature. Upwardly sloping brows signify ambition, while tufted ones indicate pleasure in hurting others. Downwardly sloping brows represent a lack of energy and a tendency to whine. Widely spaced brows show refinement and adaptability, whereas close ones denote a hot temper, energy, and determination.

The eyes

The eyes are considered to be such an important feature that "good" eyes can mitigate the effects of poor features. Eyes that dart about restlessly belong to a dishonest person, and someone who cannot meet your eyes is cunning. (I have also noticed that these darting eyes denote a lack of self-confidence and sometimes also craziness.)

Crow's feet around the eyes in an older person suggest the ability to solve problems, while in a young person they denote laziness. A person who has no fold in the eyelid will overreact to emotional situations, while someone who has the white showing all around the eye either has a severe thyroid problem—or a cunning, untrustworthy, and bad-tempered personality. Oval eyes suggest a good temper and a sharp mind, while round ones indicate a nature that is naïve and trusting. Slanted eyes denote secretiveness and a sly nature, as do narrowed eyes. Eyes that are wide apart signify openness and tolerance, while eyes that are close together suggest intolerance and a fairly tough attitude to the self and to others. Protuberant eyes denote creativity but also laziness, and deep-set eyes indicate tenacity but a lack of creativity. Small eyes indicate materialism, greed, a money-minded nature, a love of luxury and a person who will do anything or put up with anything for an easy and comfortable life. Alternatively, small eyes can indicate good concentration and the ability to finish whatever the person starts.

GRAPHOLOGY

Graphology, or the art of reading handwriting, is unique among divinations because the establishment accepts it. The police and legal profession use handwriting experts to check on forgeries, while firms the world over use them to check out prospective employees. There are even graphologists who specialize in analyzing ancient documents both in order to date them or translate them, and these experts can also tell which ancient scripts were written by the same person or otherwise.

The appearance of the page

Messy writing denotes a messy mind, but this may be a temporary situation brought on by stress. First drafts of anything are usually messy because the writer is not considering the appearance of his work but simply getting his thoughts down quickly. A person whose writing has remained unchanged since he was at school has not developed his personality or achieved any measure of individuality. The more handwriting changes after it has first been learned, the more developed the individual's personality.

Margins
If the margins are even, the subject has a tidy mind and an artistic eye. If the left margin is narrow, he is reserved and hypersensitive, while if the right margin is narrow he is generous and reckless. A page that is absolutely covered by writing either suggests stinginess or a person who has a lot to say. A page with extremely wide margins indicates a fearful, repressed and fastidious personality. A strange, ragged left margin warns of temporary insanity.

Direction
If the writing line wanders upwards the subject is optimistic and healthy at the time of writing. If it slopes downwards, he is either pessimistic or sick. If each word rides upwards he is happy, if it falls downwards he is unhappy.

Spacing
If the spacing between words is wide, the subject wants to keep others at a distance. If it is very close together he may be possessive, clinging or hostile.

Size

It is normal for a younger person to have large writing, but in an older person it means that he is either immature or that he wishes to impress people and to impose his personality on them. Small writing indicates that the writer has a reserved, introverted nature and the academic, detailed mind of a researcher. If the writing increases in size as it goes along, the subject has an open nature and he will be tactless. If it decreases in size, he is secretive and he may be a liar.

Shape

Wide writing belongs to an active, outgoing person who loves to travel but who has little consideration for others. Lean writing belongs to a pedantic person who appreciates work that is well thought out. Square writing belongs to a mathematical type and round writing indicates sociability and a loving nature. Connected writing indicates a logical mind while disconnected writing denotes an artistic and intuitive mind.

The slant

People with upright writing are organized, sensible and responsible as well as sociable and pleasant. They will help themselves and also others when asked. A slight slant to the right shows that the subject needs people in his life. He is also outgoing and extroverted if the writing is large, although more introverted if it is medium or small. A right slant also indicates a good head for business. A great deal of right slant shows that the subject is easily bored, restless and that he has many acquaintances. A slight left slant suggests that the subject is thoughtful, introspective, and slightly introverted. A good deal of left slant shows too much vulnerability and introspection. This person is a dreamer and he is very loyal to those whom he loves.

Zones

Graphologists divide letters into three zones.

Upper zone
Middle zone
Lower zone

The upper zone is formed by the loops or lines that reach upward in such letters as D, H, L, K, and T. The middle zone is formed by the main area of script, and the lower zone is formed by the tails of letters such as G, P, Y and Z.

The upper zone gives us an insight into the subject's dreams, ambitions, ideals, aims and spiritual aspirations. The middle zone concerns daily life, relationships, work and general social behavior. The lower zone relates to sex and other basic requirements such as food and security. This can also relate to physical movement (as in sports) and such things as possessiveness, acquisitiveness and materialism.

The upper zone

Average: The subject's aims and ambitions, dreams and outlooks are normal.

Tall: The subject is interested in intellectual pursuits, he is idealistic and he may be impractical and out of touch with reality. He will also be vain, proud and sensitive to criticism.

Short: The subject is practical, interested in mundane daily life and he rarely looks beyond the obvious. He is mentally alert but unable to apply his ideas.

Loops: Loops on letters such as H, D, and L denote creative thought. Straight lines suggest either a more practical and logical type of person or a person who may be temporarily stifling his creativity.

The middle zone

Large: The subject seeks to impress others and he is keen to have their approval. He is sociable, practical, and avoids acting on instinct. (He or she may also simply be young.)

Small: This subject is an instinctive, academic type who works to his own standards and does not seek approval or to impress others.

The lower zone

Large: The subject is a physical person who is interested in sports, gardening or sex. He has plenty of energy and may be rash and self-opinionated.

Loops: If the loops are wide, the subject will be aggressive, combative and materialistic. If they are angular, he could be angry, obstreperous and difficult or he could have sexual problems. Straight lines instead of loops indicate a person who is moody and unhappy, who hates physical activity and is lazy and apt to speak in short sentences or not have much to say. Alternatively, this person might be artistic, musical, or mechanical.

The I's have it

I   *A clear-thinking person who is interested in mechanics and engineering*

I   *The concise type who deals only with essentials*

l   *This subject is either self-important or very intellectual*

Y   *A physical, outdoor type of person*

∩   *This one avoids responsibility*

g   *A bit full of himself, but otherwise reasonable*

g   *Pleasant and humorous with an open, friendly nature*

Capital letters

Large capitals indicate a big ego and small ones suggest a small one. Ornamental capitals belong to someone who is vain or who is an unusual personality. Capitals that lean all over the rest of the writing show an aggressive and fussy personality.

A A   *This A shows kindness and sympathy*

A A   *This A shows balance and common sense*

B   *This closed B will not be taken in or swindled by others*

B   *This open B is gullible*

D E   *These lead-in strokes show an aggressive, irritable, impatient nature, a person who is proud and status-conscious*

C E I   *Good mentality, freedom loving and idealistic. A quick thinker with good judgment*

P R   *Broken capitals show open-mindedness and generosity*

P R *Closed capitals show a cautious, cheapskate nature*

M *"Painted" letters show an artistic nature*

Lower-case letters

a a *Big-heartedness, generosity and a nature that is too open*

a o *Secretiveness and the ability to keep confidences*

a c s *The lead-in stroke shows petulance and irritability—also a person who is slow to warm up sexually*

b b *The open b shows generosity and gullibility; the closed one is cautious and tightfisted*

g *Literary ability and a quick mind*

d d *A loop on the d shows sensitive feelings, while the lack of a loop indicates a person who does not worry about other people's opinion of him*

t t *The same as for the d above*

f t *A loop missing on the f shows a sound mind. Two loops missing suggest that the subject is artistic and clever with his hands*

h k *An angular h can indicate aggression or a sharp intellect, while an angular k is always a sign of an aggressive personality*

m n w *Rounded letters denote gentleness and also someone who is good with his hands*

m n w *Angular writing belongs to the type of person who has an active mind, a love of efficiency and who is enthusiastic about what he does*

p p *An open p belongs to a straightforward person who is gentle and who enjoys the simple things of life. A loop on the down-stroke shows that the subject wants to be more mobile or to get out of doors more than he does*

This represents a proud, awkward person
A gentle, thoughtful person
When the r looks like a printed letter, the subject is clever and versatile

A quick mind with many interests and no lack of ability. Also a tenacious person who will not be pushed around

The closed s denotes great caution

A yielding nature

Wide loops—this person is over-emotional, histrionic and hysterical. Possibly also a good actor

Narrow loops indicate suppressed emotion

Lines instead of loops denote good judgment and a head that rules the heart. A rapid thinker who probably has a good education

Tiny lower loops signify a lack of vitality

Large lower loops show a vital person who enjoys exercise, sports or dancing

Angular loops demonstrate determination and forcefulness

Large angular loops signify a tendency to exaggerate, be pompous and boastful and to enjoy ordering people around

No loops at all show a mind that rules the heart and a mental rather than a physical personality

A multiplication of loops shows temporary or permanent insanity. This person may be a liar or a deceiver and will not be popular

Flicks instead of loops denote a person who is persnickety about appearances, fussy and petty-minded about small matters

Signatures

Very often the signature is different from other handwriting. There may also be different names or different ways of signing things according to what it is. For example I use a small, right-slant "S. Fenton" scrawl for checks, credit cards, official matters, and so forth where formality is important. This is the signature that I used before becoming a writer and celebrity. I habitually use a middle-sized, upright and clearly written "Sasha Fenton" for business letters, signing books or anything to do with my work. In the first case, this is for convenience, while in the second case, I guess I am saying, "this is who I am and this is what I do". If my personality were less important to my work, I probably wouldn't have instinctively chosen to use such a signature.

If the signature is clearly legible, the subject is honest and open. If it is illegible, he may be hiding something or he may just be shy. If the forename is larger and more strongly emphasized, he will want to put things on a personal basis but if the surname is emphasized, he will want to keep things formal. A dot after the signature shows a tidy mind, but also the need for approval or to impress others. A line below shows self-importance but it will be put there unconsciously in some cases to compensate for the lack of lower-loop letters in the signature. Embellishments are put there to draw attention to the subject and to show how special he is.

A signature with a soft appearance denotes a gentle personality, while a more angular or aggressive one shows a tougher and more difficult personality. A line that leads into the signature shows that the subject is clinging to the past while a line that tails out at the end shows tact, kindness or generosity. If the signature is placed in the middle of the page or to the left, the subject is shy or introverted; if it is on the right, he is cheerful and outgoing.

MOLES

Years ago people considered that the position of a mole on the body signified certain characteristics of a person and also a particular kind of outlook for the future. I have reproduced the ideas in this chapter from an early 19th century script that clearly has roots that go back much further than that. After checking out people and their moles, I have to say that most of this stuff is pretty silly—but annoyingly, some of it is quite accurate. Please don't take the more frightening interpretations literally, but simply have a bit of fun with this rather foolish form of divination.

The size, color, and shape of the mole must be taken into consideration, because while a collection of pale freckles won't mean anything, an isolated and obvious mole will. The larger the mole, the more important it is. If a mole is round, its effects will be beneficial. An oblong mole is fairly lucky but an angular one is considered to be a bad omen. A dark mole has a stronger effect than a pale one. A very hairy one is considered to be a very bad omen indeed, while a couple of hairs on a mole bring prosperity.

- I have noticed within my own family that moles are often an inherited characteristic and that family members will often have similar moles in similar positions.
- I hardly need to add that if a mole becomes itchy, crusty or starts to spread you must visit your doctor immediately, as this could be an indication of skin cancer.

Location of Moles

1. A mole on the right side of the forehead shows that the person is going places in his career.
2. On the right eyebrow, the subject will marry when young and his or her partner will be very pleasant to live with.
3. On the left side of either the forehead or the eyebrow, unexpected disappointment.
4. A mole on the outside corner of either eye denotes that the subject is steady, sober and reliable. Tradition says that he may suffer a violent death.
5. A mole on either cheek means that the subject will never be rich but he won't be particularly poor either.
6. A mole on the nose suggests success in all undertakings.
7. One on the lip means that the subject is stylish and fastidious and also lucky in matters of love.

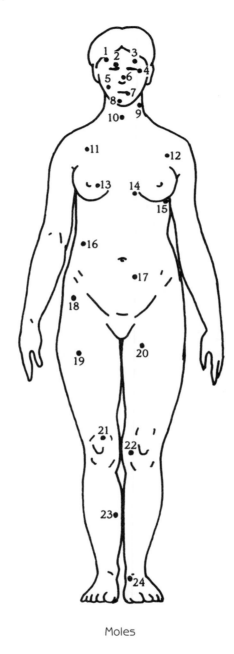

Moles

8. On the chin, this shows luck and success in career and business matters. This person will reach a position of great status.
9. A mole on the neck means that the subject will narrowly avoid being suffocated. After this event, the subject will receive a large unexpected legacy and rise to a position of great status.
10. A mole on the throat indicates wealth acquired through marriage.

11. On the right side of the chest or back, a mole indicates fall in status and income. This also suggests that most of the subject's children will be girls.

12. On the left side of the chest or back, a mole indicates success in business and a high level of sexuality. Most of this subject's children will be boys. (This one definitely doesn't work!)

13. A woman with a mole on her breast will have a mediocre life with no great gains or losses.

14. A man with a mole on the left side of the chest over the heart denotes a kindly person who likes to ramble on. He is often slightly discontented, as he tends to chew things over too much in his mind.

15. In a woman, a mole under the left breast suggests that she will carry and give birth to children without difficulty.

16. A mole, which is low down on the right side of the ribs, suggests a slow thinker who is best left to do things at his own pace.

17. A mole on the belly belongs to a selfish, greedy, gluttonous and lazy person. This subject is also slovenly and dirty.

18. A mole that is fairly low down on the back means a lifetime of hard work. (I have discovered that this one is absolutely true, as everyone I have encountered who works hard seems to have such a mole.)

19. A mole on the hip means that the person will have many children who will be patient, hardworking and who will turn out to be a credit to him.

20. On the right thigh, riches plus a happy and lucky marriage.

21. On the left thigh, poverty and a lack of friends. This subject is also on the receiving end of hatred and injustice from others.

22. On the right knee, an easy life and a good marriage.

23. On the left knee, a temper that can result in rash acts, but under normal circumstances a cool, honest and decent person.

24. On either calf, a lazy thoughtless person who lives for today and who doesn't think forward.

25. A mole on either ankle suggests that a male subject will be somewhat feminine or even effeminate in his manner, while a female will be courageous, active and a real shrew!

ITCHES

We all know that when one of our ears is itching or burning it means that someone is talking about us or that when our right palm itches that money is on the way. However, we are not as familiar with other "itchy" wives' tales and other similar physical omens.

Most itches are momentary things that go away as quickly as they come and have no special significance, but some need to be taken seriously. In fact, any persistent itch deserves a visit to the doctor. For example, regular episodes of itching or burning in the feet (especially during the night) can be a symptom of diabetes. Ongoing itchiness on the arms and legs can also signal diabetes. A persistent itch on the back (towards the lower end of the left shoulder blade) can denote heart disease. A pregnant woman with a severe and constant itch on her hands must seek immediate medical advice. If her doctor doesn't take her worries seriously, she must insist on consulting a specialist, because this kind of itch can indicate a condition that causes stillbirth. However, please use common sense here, as the occasional itch or other bodily event usually means nothing—apart from the amusing meanings given in the following list.

1. If the crown of your head itches, promotion and an increase in salary are on the way.
2. If you comb your hair and find it coming out in large amounts, you will soon be seriously ill. (This has a basis in fact because when sickness looms, the body sheds hair in a kind of energy-saving campaign.)
3. If your right eyebrow itches, you will soon meet up again with an old friend or be reunited with a previous lover.
4. If your left eyebrow itches, you will soon meet a friend who is sick or you will see your old lover with someone else.
5. A ringing in your right ear means that you will soon hear good news.
6. A ringing in your left ear means that you will soon hear bad news. When your left ear tingles, someone is maligning your name.
7. A violent itching of the nose means that trouble and worry is on the way. (Or hay fever perhaps?)
8. Itchy lips mean that someone is speaking badly of you behind your back.
9. An itch on the back of your neck means that someone close to you is about to suffer a violent death. (Don't take this one seriously!)
10. An itchy right shoulder means that you will shortly receive a large legacy.
11. An itchy left shoulder means that you will soon be weighed down with troubles.
12. If your right elbow itches, good news is on the way.

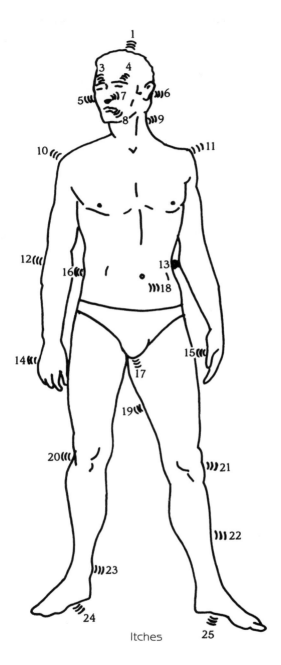

Itches

13. If your left elbow itches, you will suffer a disappointment.
14. If your right palm is itchy, there is money on its way to you.
15. If your left palm itches, you will have to pay someone else's debts.
16. An itchy spine denotes that you will soon bear heavy burdens.

17. An itching of the genital region means that you will shortly have an addition to your family, or that you will be married shortly.
18. If your tummy itches, you can expect to eat a sumptuous meal.
19. If one or both of your thighs itch, you will soon be sleeping elsewhere.
20. If your right knee itches, your life will change for the better and you will become interested in some kind of religion.
21. If your left knee itches, you will have a setback in life.
22. If your shins itch, you will have a long and painful illness. (Another one that is not worth taking seriously!)
23. If your ankle joints itch, you will be united or reunited with a loved one. If you are already happily settled, your life will become even happier.
24. If the sole of your right foot itches, you will soon go on a pleasant journey.
25. If the sole of your left foot itches, you will soon go on a sad or unpleasant journey.
26. Finally, if you find yourself unaccountably depressed, you will soon be hearing some good news.

PENDLING AND DOWSING

Divining rods and pendulums are usually used to locate things, but they can also be used in order to discover a straight "yes" or "no" answer to a question. Rods can be used to find underground sources of water, drain pipes, sources of specific minerals and lost objects. A pendulum can be used to identify an illness or spot a dietary deficiency. Rods and pendulums can be held over a map or a sketch of a specific place in order to find someone or something.

Preparation and Ritual

Before using a new pendulum or set of dowsing rods, hold them in your hands and ask your spiritual guides to help you to use them in a caring and truthful manner. Imagine yourself calling down a shaft of white light from the universe, mentally allow this to settle around your feet and then wind it up around your body in a clockwise direction.

Once you have prepared your rods or pendulum, you will have to establish which kind of movement will be your "yes" and which will be your "no." If using dowsing rods, hold them out in front of you at a comfortable distance from your body and think "yes." If the rods cross, this will be your "yes" or if they part then that will be your "yes." If you are using a pendulum, wind the string or chain around your little finger and hold your hand with the palm uppermost. Then allow the chain to run across the underside of your fingers and then down over your index finger. Now think "yes." The pendulum may move backwards, side to side or in a circle. The movement will be in direct response to your brain patterns and nerve endings, because the pendulum and you are merely channels for your guides to use. The pendulum does not have any life itself, other than the receptive energy that you charged it with when you went through the preparation ritual. After doing this, go through the same exercise again, this time thinking "no," and this will give you your "no" movement. You can now form a question in your mind, but remember to couch this in such a manner as to receive a straight "yes" or "no" answer.

If you are trying to identify an ailment, you can draw a sketch of the sick person and dowse over this with a pendulum. Start by holding the pendulum over the head and slowly draw it down the body, and the area of the body that is sick will set off a movement in the pendulum. Dowsing for allergies is a more specific divination because you will need to buy a book that shows exactly what length of thread your pendulum needs to be held at in order to discover what it is that the person is allergic to.

Another way to dowse for a specific sickness is to write a list of the most likely ailments, leaving plenty of space between the words. Then take your pendulum and dowse over the list, and if the person has one of the ailments on the list, the pendulum will register your "yes" position.

Ley Lines

You may have read that there are specific energy lines called ley lines that cross a country, but there are many minor ley lines as well. If you suspect that the position that you sleep in or that your desk is placed in doesn't suit you, you can dowse for a negative line in that area. Simply take your rods and think "ley line." If the rods find one, they will cross. Now do it again, thinking "negative ley line" and if the rods cross again, you know that is what you have discovered. Simply moving your bed, desk, chair or other piece of furniture to a different part of the room or to a different room could improve your life.

Other Things

Just as you can dowse over a list of ailments, so can you dowse over a list of any other kind. If you have several choices to make or if you want to know the answer to anything, just write a variety of answers down on a piece of paper, leaving plenty of space between the lines and then dowse over them. The right choice or the answer to your question will set the pendulum into action. If you find rods easier to use than a pendulum, then simply write each choice or answer on separate pieces of paper and lay them around the floor. Then dowse over the pieces of paper with your rods and see which one activates the rods. If none of them do, try a different set of answers.

THE MEANING OF DREAMS

Scientists tell us that we dream every time we sleep. Sleep deepens and lightens in fairly fixed periods with ninety minutes of deep sleep, interspersed with blocks of fifteen or twenty minutes of lighter sleep. Dreaming is the mind's way of sifting the impressions with which it has been bombarded throughout the day, keeping those that are relevant and rejecting those that are not. If a natural pattern of dreaming is essential to mental health, then it is obvious that any drug that interferes with this could cause some kind of side effect.

It is worth looking for a logical reason for a bad dream before jumping to the conclusion that it means something ominous. It used to be said that eating cheese before going to bed caused bad dreams! Certainly too much alcohol or food can give one a bad night, while pain or a high temperature are bound to disturb one's sleep. Every now and then a dream will keep coming back to haunt us over a period of several weeks, and in this case there is definitely something significant to consider.

Many dream meanings tell us something about our state of mind, perhaps bringing to our attention things that are at the back of our minds that we don't wish to consciously acknowledge. I remember someone telling me that she was superficially happy to be planning her wedding and looking forward to being married to her fiancé, but every night she dreamed that she was locked away in prison. This woman's subconscious was clearly telling her that she was getting herself into a difficult situation that would be hard to escape from—and it turned out to be true.

Stress dreams can include going somewhere only to find that we have forgotten something vital, or trying to get into a car and not being able to, or perhaps trying to stop a car that is rolling down the street. There are many variations of these and they all relate to stress in some way. Many dreams are known as contrary dreams, which means that a bad dream may actually be an indication of good fortune being on the way.

Occult significance

Of course, there are dreams that have a specific occult significance. These might warn of a forthcoming problem or predict a particular event. Before the Arab terrorists crashed their airplanes into the World Trade Center, many psychic and sensitive people had dreams about it—and I was one of them. There may be a symbolic dream that hides a specific meaning. A common example is dreaming of a broken wedding ring, which signifies uncertainty about a marriage or relationship.

Health

The Chinese believe that certain kinds of dreams indicate particular health problems. For instance, they believe that dreams of terror indicate heart problems, while dreams of bloodshed relate to the lungs. Dreaming of hacking one's way through the jungle signifies liver problems and dreaming of sharp pain indicates kidney disorders. Dreams of some kind of repetitious action, such as swinging backwards and forwards signify anemia. A single dream of this kind is probably fairly meaningless, but if a dream recurs or persists, then it might be worth taking it seriously and having a checkup.

Examples of dream meanings

The following list shows some traditional dream interpretations. This is a purely divinatory list and doesn't take any kind of deep psychological meaning into account. Although this kind of divination is only meant for fun, I have found it to work quite well. There are plenty of books that cover every conceivable kind of dream. Books dedicated to the subject will also give longer interpretations to the dreams than I offer here.

Dream interpretation list

Dreams about babies

Baby
Good luck for the dreamer and his family.

Birth
Good fortune.

Cradle
Hopes and wishes will be fulfilled.

Pregnancy
Good news is on the way.

Dreams about marriage

Bells
Good news.

Bouquet
Slight disappointment.

Horseshoe
A pleasant journey.

Wedding
Joy and happiness lie ahead.

Dreams of death

These are extremely common, and different sources give different interpretations, but most seem to consider them lucky, although some are not. Death in many occult beliefs indicates a fresh start or the transformation of something that is ready to die off and evolve into something new and better.

Burial
The dreamer will soon be married.

Cemetery
The dreamer will hear of a death.

Death
Turning point, transformation, good fortune, and happiness.

Gallows
Prosperity.

Shipwreck
Hesitation and disappointments.

Tomb
A long happy life foretold.

Dreams about men

Doctor
Illness is on the way.

Friend
Good luck and happiness.

Horseman
Plans fulfilled.

Lawyer
A warning of legal or financial difficulties.

Old man
Happiness for the family.

Policeman
Peace and safety.

Postman
Long-awaited news.

Sailor
Difficulties or delays in plans.

Dreams about women

Actress
Deception by those you trust.

Empress
Both status and success or pride causes a fall.

Nun
Peace of mind.

Witch
Difficulties in the near future.

Dreams about friends

Drowning friend
Someone will render the dreamer a service.

Friend's house
Good luck in work and other plans.

Friend in difficulty
Either your friend will need help, or you will need your friend to help you.

Dreams about children

Children playing
Happiness is on the way.

Crying child
A wish will be fulfilled.

Dancing child
Difficulties ahead.

Death of a child
A welcome visitor.

Sleeping child
Good luck is coming to the dreamer.

Dreams about animals, birds, insects, and fish

Ants
Hard work ahead, but the results will be worthwhile.

Bat
Danger threatens.

Bear
Disagreements with friends.

Bees
Prosperity and progress.
NB: While every source I have come across agrees with the above interpretation, I once heard a dream interpretation specialist tell a woman that dreaming of bees meant hav-

ing a difficult mother-in-law. The woman agreed emphatically that this was so in her case!

Cat
Beware of treachery.

Cockerel
Success and joy are on the way.

Cow
Prosperity.

Crab
A parting.

Dog
Malicious gossip.

Donkey
Trouble in store.

Dove
Peace and happiness in love.

Duck
A stranger brings bad news.

Eagle
Success.

Elephant
Plans will succeed.

Fish
Unexpected news.

Fox
Plans will succeed beyond your wildest expectations.

Goose
Someone who you love will let you down.

Hedgehog
Business difficulties and complications.

Hen
Celebrations and parties.

Horse
Black horse: Disappointments.
Brown horse: Stagnation and delays.
White horse: Financial progress.

Lamb
Wishes will come true.

Lion
You will soon take the lead in an important enterprise.

Parrot
A trusted friend will quarrel with you.

Peacock
Wealth coming through the family.

Rabbit
You will soon make a good and useful friend.

Rat
A supposed friend is working against you. Women should beware of becoming entangled with a "rat".

Snake
Gossip. However, this is good news for love affairs.

Spider
Danger of being involved in a quarrel.

Swallow
Domestic circumstances will change a little.

Swan
Financial progress and happiness.

Tiger
Hidden danger threatens. (Oddly enough, tigers tend to feature when we have a high temperature, so this could indicate the onset of influenza or a similar illness.)

Toad
Hidden danger.

Vulture
Illness in the family.

Wolf
Business losses and worries.

Worms
A number of small worries.

Dreams about conditions

Applause
A friend will rebuke the dreamer.

Attack
Rashness will cause difficulties.

Battle
Health worries.

Climbing
Success coming, albeit slowly.

Competition

It will soon be easier to attain ambitions.

Dancing
Pleasure, parties, and dancing.

Dispute
Take care; be cautious.

Exile
Loss of something or someone valuable.

Falling
A confusing time is ahead.

Finding money
Loss.

Flying
Advancement in circumstances and/or a desire to escape.

Following one's own funeral
Turning point, transformation, great and lasting success.

Gambling
Success will be coming soon.

Honors
Beware of slander.

Imprisonment
Delays and problems that are hard to resolve. This could also be a warning against getting into a difficult situation in the near future.

Kidnapping
Success in plans.

Legacy
Financial loss.

Murder
Successful outcome in plans.

Nakedness
Financial loss.

Poverty
Change for the better.

Presents
Loss that wipes out previous gains.

Reading
Pleasure coming from a new source.

Screaming
Bad news is coming.

Shopping
Unexpected benefits are coming.

Singing
Success in endeavors.

Suicide
Upheaval and major changes.

Swimming
Improvement after a bad period of time.

Travel
Friends will let the dreamer down.

Undressing
Lack of foresight will cause problems.

Visiting
A grave injustice is on the way.

Wealth
Disillusionment.

Weeping
Good news is on the way.

Wrestling
The dreamer will win in the end.

Writing
Danger of offending a friend.

Dreams about money

Finding money
Difficulties are on the way.

Losing money
Plans will succeed beyond the dreamer's wildest hopes.

Counting money
Gains are coming.

Spending money
Losses are on the way.

Dreams about health

Amputation
Slights and injustices.

Asthma
Difficulties are ahead.

Burns
Success coming; an end of troubles.

Loss of a tooth
Loss of a friend or relative.

Problems with feet
Prosperity.

Problems with hands
Parting from a good friend.

Ulcer
Temporary difficulty.

General dream list

Airplane
Ambition to be fulfilled.

Ambulance
Illness in the family.

Axe
Help from a friend.

Bag
Full: Prosperity.
Empty: Hard times ahead.

Ball
Great moves forward.

Bank
Money worries.

Barrel
Full: Improvement in circumstances.
Empty: Money worries.

Basket
A welcome invitation.

Bath
Happiness to come.

Beans
Danger to the family.

Bed
If made: Rest.
If unmade: Take care, avoid trouble.

Bell
Good news, joy.

Blood
An accident.

Boat
News, a successful journey.

Bridge
Troubles will soon pass.

Buttons
Peace and joy in the family.

Candle
Lit: A birth in the family.
Extinguished: A death in the dreamer's circle.

Castle
Unexpectedly pleasurable event.

Chain
Difficulties.

Church
Peace after a period of trouble.

Clock
Business matters that require the dreamer's attention.

Clouds
Quarrels with friends.

Coal
The dreamer will impress his superiors.

Cottage
Health and happiness.

Crown
Honors.

Crossroads
Important decisions to be made.

Dice
Beware of taking a gamble, as losses are possible.

Dungeon
Danger for those around the dreamer.

Earthquake
Someone close to you is running a risk.

Eggs
An upturn in finances; also good health.

Eyes
A lover is on the way or the dreamer's current love life will improve.

Eyeglasses
The dreamer's self-esteem will take a knock.

Factory
The dreamer's efforts will be rewarded.

Fingers
Litigation concerning money.

Fire
Unexpected happy event.

Fireplace
Someone will go away.

Flag
A change in life brings success.

Flowers
A trip or a move to the countryside.

Fountain
A busy time is ahead.

Glass
Full: The dreamer will soon hear from a loved one.
Empty: Temporary difficulties.
Broken: Wishes will come true. If appropriate, a wedding.

Globe
A worthwhile journey.

Gun
Danger, disappointment, or limited success.

Hammer
Recklessness will cause problems.

Hand
The dreamer will be surrounded by flatterers.

Hat
Disappointment.

House
This shows the state of the dreamer's mind. The house in the dream will probably be different from the one he lives in. The condition of the house in the dream should be taken into consideration. For instance, is it large, small, tidy, messy, lonely, or filled with partygoers? What kinds of emotions are prevalent in the dream?

Island
Loneliness to come.

Jewels
A raise in status and an upturn in finances.

Key
The dreamer must prepare for any upcoming interview so that he makes the best of himself.

Kitchen
Improvement in finances. Like the house dream, the state of the kitchen reflects the state of the dreamer's mind.

Knife
Danger for the dreamer or for a loved one.

Knot
Complications in affairs.

Ladder
Patience will bring success.

Lamp
Lit: Good for business affairs.
Extinguished: Concealment of something important from the dreamer.

Lighthouse
Good advice is on the way.

Linen (dirty)
Arguments in the family—don't air secrets in public.

Lock
Guard against theft.

Map
Long journey.

Meat
Raw: Prosperity.
Cooked: Disappointment.

Mirror
Flattery from the opposite sex.

Milk
In a glass or jug: Tranquility.
Spilt: Plans will not work out.

Moon
Something will work out within a month.

Mountain
Work brings rewards. Improvements in affairs.

Music
Happy times ahead.

Nails
Metal: Hard work is ahead. Difficulties to overcome.
Fingernails: Quarrels and financial difficulties.

Necklace
Happiness and fun.

Nest
A windfall.

Net
Financial improvement and a raise in status.

Nuts
Problems will soon be solved.

Oak tree
Parting from a friend.

Opals
Happiness in love.

Oranges
Happiness and pleasure.

Palace
Sorrow for a friend.

Palm tree
The dreamer's dearest wish will come true.

Pin
Guard against a loss of status or a loss of face.

Pipe
An argument.

Plow
Respect and reward for good work.

Pond
Stagnation in affairs.

Purse
Full: Slight loss.
Empty: Unexpected gain.

Race
The dreamer will soon be ahead of others.

Rainbow
A brighter future.

Razor
A quarrel brings unhappiness.

Road
Work brings rewards.

Rocks
Temporary difficulties.

Rose
Social success.

Scissors
A quarrel and the loss of a friend.

Sea
Calm: Happiness.
Stormy: Anger.

Shooting star
Success in every way.

Sky
Wishes will shortly be fulfilled.
Night sky: Temporary difficulties.
Stormy sky: Great changes in the dreamer's way of life.

Smoke
A bad business transaction incurring losses.

Stairs
Improvement and change in circumstances.

Sun
Success in exams, business, or anything else.

Sword
Success, but the dreamer must guard against jealousy or attack by others.

Table
Improvement in health.

Tent
Unaccustomed activities.

Thorn
The dreamer will bring unhappiness to another.

Thunder
Danger for the dreamer or a loved one.

Tower
Ambitions will be achieved.

Train station
A journey.

Trees
Upright: Ambitions achieved.
Felled or fallen: Parting from a loved one.

Treasure
Hopes will come to nothing.

Tunnel
Extreme danger. Someone close to the dreamer may be dying or there could be a real threat to the dreamer's health or life.

Umbrella
Open: Friends will be helpful.
Closed: Prosperity in business.

Violin
Affairs of love will go well.

Volcano
Upheavals. Physical effort will need to be made.

Water
Clear: Good health and prosperity.
Muddy: Danger from disputes.
Hot: Unexpected danger.

Wheel
Change for the better. A journey.

Window
Open: Problems will be solved.
Closed: Unexpected danger, but the dreamer should be safe.

Wine
Social events and celebrations.

Yacht
Improvement in status and changes for the better.

TEA AND COFFEE READING

The art of reading tea leaves or coffee grounds used to be very popular, but it went out of fashion for several years, as did playing card reading, and this was probably due to the massive rise in popularity of the Tarot as a means of telling fortunes. However, teacup reading is slowly creeping back into people's consciousness once again. There are books that cover every possible symbol. However, in the meantime, the following list shows many of the more obvious symbols—which should suffice for the beginner.

Preparation

Use a teacup and saucer rather than a mug or a small demitasse cup. A shallow cup with a plain interior is best, because patterns or a fluted shape will interfere with the reading. Ask your questioner to drink the tea or coffee and then to swirl the remaining material around in the cup in an counter-clockwise direction three times, using his left hand. Then ask him to gently place the cup upside down on the saucer. Either you or the questioner should now slowly turn the cup three times in an counter-clockwise direction, once again using the left hand.

Needless to say, you will need to use leaf tea rather than tea bags—and ground coffee rather than instant. There are no rules about the type of tea or coffee you choose to use but perhaps the types with the larger leaves or grounds would be best. Herbal tea, fruit tea or any kind of tea or coffee will work perfectly well if that is what you or your questioner prefers to drink.

After this, turn the cup over, keeping the handle towards you, tilt it to a convenient angle and take a good look inside.

Location and timing of events

The illustration on page 112 shows the "geography" of the cup. The handle represents the questioner himself. Any leaves in that area of the cup show that events concerning him will occur in or near his home. The opposite side of the cup refers to strangers and events that occur away from home.

Symbols that point towards the handle represent things that are approaching the questioner, while those that point away from him indicate things that are moving away from him. This movement might be a matter of location, or it may be a matter of timing. The bottom of the cup shows sorrows and the top shows joys.

The rim of the cup represents the near future. The area halfway down signifies events that will occur within a few weeks or months, while the area close to the bottom suggests the more distant future. If there are any numbers visible, these may help with the timing of events. For instance, an anchor would suggest a journey, and if the number three accompanied this, it would tell of a journey to come in three month's time.

Some teacup lore

- If two full spoons are accidentally put into one saucer, there will be news of twins.
- If a spoon is accidentally placed upside down on a saucer, there will be news of a close relative becoming sick.
- A single leaf floating on a full cup of liquid means that the questioner will come into money.
- A single leaf that is stuck at the side of a full cup of liquid indicates that a stranger will soon enter the questioner's life.
- Stalks represent people. The color and size of the stalk can be assessed for an indication of the general appearance of the person.
- Letters of the alphabet can indicate people's names.
- A triangle is usually considered to be lucky. But if it is found at the bottom of the cup or with the apex pointing downwards, there may be a spell of bad luck on the way, or perhaps something that has been all right up to now could suddenly become difficult.
- Squares represent protection or restriction. If a dangerous symbol, such as an arrow, appears inside a square, the questioner will be protected from harm.
- Crosses denote sadness or troubles to be faced.
- Dots always symbolize money. If the dots are close to another symbol, they may be linked.
- When a mountain appears, the questioner will soon need to make a major effort in life.
- Clouds indicate muddles and illusion.
- Clear straight lines denote happy journeys, while wavy or broken ones signify problems related to travel.
- If you are hoping to find a new lover, place a teaspoon in a saucer and drip liquid into it until the spoon is full, while counting the number of drips that this takes. The number of drips will tell you how many months will go by before you find your new lover.

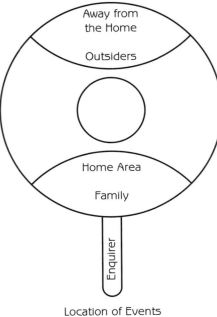

Away from
the Home

Outsiders

Home Area

Family

Enquirer

Location of Events

Very Near Future

Few months' time

Distant future

Enquirer

Timing of Events

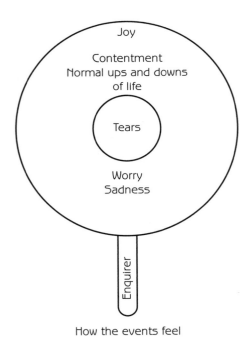

Joy

Contentment
Normal ups and downs
of life

Tears

Worry
Sadness

Enquirer

How the events feel

The Symbols

Acorn
The start of something that will grow and succeed. A long life and good fortune. If the acorn is in the middle of the cup, this indicates an improvement in health; other positions mean an improvement in finances.

Airplane
Sudden journeys for the questioner or someone close to him. If the airplane is ascending, things are on the up-and-up, but if it is descending there will be unexpected trouble. If the plane is traveling towards the questioner it may be that someone is traveling to see him.

Anchor
A good symbol. If it is near the rim of the cup, there will be success in career and true love. A wish will come true soon. If halfway down, a journey will be successful. If there are dots around the anchor, this is very lucky indeed. If it is at the bottom of the cup, the questioner will receive help from friends and overcome difficulties. Only if the symbol is partially covered does it indicate continued troubles.

Angel
Good news, signifying love, happiness, and peace. There may be spiritual help on the way. Any new project (especially the birth of a child) will be accompanied by good luck. If the symbol is close to the handle of the cup, the home area will be particularly happy.

Arch
A happy marriage, a fresh start and unexpected benefits. A proposal of marriage is possible, while other pleasant but temporary situations may become permanent.

Apple
A time of achievement, happiness, and success. Hopes and wishes will be fulfilled. If it is at the bottom of the cup, over-indulgence or temptation.

Arrow
Bad news. If the arrow points towards the handle, bad news is coming to the questioner. If it points away, the questioner may be the bearer of bad news. Dots show that financial trouble is ahead.

Baby
This may indicate the birth of a child but also the birth of a new project. If at the bottom of the cup the pregnancy or plans may miscarry.

Bag
If closed, the questioner will be caught in a trap; if open he will manage to escape.

Ball
Ups and downs in life. The questioner will soon bounce back from problems, and there will soon be new opportunities opening up.

Balloon
Success, but the position will show whether this is imminent or not. The closer to the top of the cup, the shorter the time scale.

Basket
Social success, happiness, and good fortune in and around the home. This is usually a good omen but an empty basket or one that is obscured by other symbols can indicate domestic problems ahead.

Bed
A neat bed signifies a tidy mind, rest, and peace. A rumpled bed suggests sleepless nights and worry.

Bees
This has a combination of meanings that are usually good. This indicates a busy time ahead, either at home, work, or both. There will be family gatherings and visitors bringing good news. One or more bees also signal good news for business ventures, money, and status at work or in business. A beehive also indicates a busy time.

Bell
This says that important news is on the way, and this can sometimes be news of a wedding. If the bell is near the rim, there will be promotion at work. If halfway up, there will be good news of a general nature. If near the bottom, there could be sad news. Two bells indicate great happiness and celebrations and any forthcoming marriage will be successful.

Bird
Flying birds mean travel and also good ideas that can be translated into money. If surrounded by a circle or a square, there may be a proposal. Standing birds suggest that plans will be held up, while birds in a group indicate business meetings. If caged, there will be obstacles and restrictions. If the bird is holding a branch there will be reconciliation. A bird's nest signifies security, and if there are eggs in it, there will be a "nest egg." A broken nest might indicate a broken home.

Boat
Protection from danger, a safe haven, or a safe journey. If the boat is capsized, there will be unreliable people and upsetting circumstances.

Book
Depending upon the circumstances, a book can indicate studies, secrets, legal matters or writing for a living.

Box
If open, a romantic problem will soon sort itself out. If closed, something that has been lost will turn up.

Broom
Indicates that it is time to clear out old problems and start afresh.

Butterfly
A fickle lover or a short-lived affair. If surrounded by dots, this will be costly.

Candle

Illumination, help from others, inspiration, enlightenment. A guttering candle says that someone close to the questioner is becoming less important to him.

Cat

If the cat is pouncing, there will be treachery and false friends. If it is seated, there will be contentment and good luck.

Chair

A time to rest, visitors; or, with dots nearby, a financial improvement.

Chimney

If smoke rises up, things will go well but if it goes sideways the questioner may soon be restricted or bored. No smoke, hidden danger.

Church

Help, safety, and unexpected benefits.

Circle or ring

This is often a sign of an impending marriage. With dots, a baby—three dots indicate a boy. Two circles signify a hasty marriage that brings regrets or perhaps two marriages.

Coffin

Sad news, regret, loss, and an enforced decision to bring something to an end. Someone may leave the questioner, but this may be a relief.

Crescent

A new interest and success in finances, a journey over water and success for or through women. Changes may come about at the time of the new moon. If the moon is accompanied by a star, this is an exceptionally lucky omen. A new moon indicates new interests and success in finances. Any crescent could indicate luck though dealings with women or travel over water.

Cross

Trouble, suffering, worry, and sad news if it is close to the rim.

Crown

Honors and success. With a star nearby, a crown suggests unexpected luck.

Cup

Success and fulfillment, especially in creative and emotional matters.

Dagger

A jealous person will make trouble. Also a warning against haste.

Devil

Passion, lust, or a hectic love affair.

Dice

If bad omens are nearby, this is a warning against gambling. Otherwise, speculation should be all right.

Dog
If the dog is running and happy, there will be happy meetings. If it is sad or at the bottom of the cup, a friend will need help.

Dot
A single dot increases the importance of any symbol near it. Otherwise dots mean money.

Dragon
Unforeseen problems, major clashes, and upheavals.

Drum
Arguments. If it is near the bottom of the cup there may be rumors and scandal attached to the questioner. Otherwise a successful career involving the general public.

Duck
Money coming, luck in gambling, or work connected to travel and foreigners.

Eagle
A change of address and a time to grasp opportunities.

Egg
A symbol of fertility. A fresh start and the birth of a project.

Elephant
A symbol of strength, wisdom and a slow climb up the ladder of success. A good time for a new business or a new lover.

Envelope
Good news is on the way. A letter or number may give you a clue as to whom this is from.

Eye
The questioner may learn something to his advantage soon, but be on guard against untrustworthy people.

Face
If this looks like someone the questioner knows, this could be significant. Otherwise the omen is good if the face is smiling, not so good if it is sad or scowling.

Fan
A warning to keep something to oneself.

Fish
This indicates luck in anything the questioner wishes to do. Travel, a move of house or a lucky meeting with a foreigner is possible.

Flag
This is a good omen if backed up by other good omens, however if the flag is black or at half-mast, courage will soon be needed.

Fork in a road
A choice of pathways is ahead.

Frog
This is associated with the ancient Egyptian goddess, Isis, and it foretells good luck, happiness, good friends, love, and protection from harm.

Gallows
The questioner's judgment may not be reliable in the near future.

Gate
An opportunity.

Grapes
Grapes are associated with the ancient Greek god, Dionysus or the Roman god, Bacchus. So a good time should soon be had by all, but the questioner will need to guard against deception.

Guitar
Social events that include music, romance and relaxation.

Gun
Quarrels, violence, war and even a threat of death by violence. If the gun is in the home area, that is where the danger will be, otherwise the questioner must guard against mugging and so on. If the gun is at the bottom of the cup, there is a real threat of death by violence, terrorism or war.

Hammer
There is much work to be done. Not all of it is pleasant but it must be tackled.

Hand
If the hand is pointing to the handle, a situation is likely to develop in the home, if it is pointing away from the handle, the situation will occur outside the home. If the hand is open, friends will be helpful, but if it shows a fist, the questioner can expect a fight. Clasped hands signify friendships and agreements, while a clenched fist at the bottom of the cup indicates that the questioner will need to keep his feelings under tight control. Thumbs up = go ahead. Thumbs down = wait.

Hat
A man's hat is an unlucky sign but a woman's hat is a fortunate one.

Heart
A symbol of love. A heart with arrows through it signifies a passionate romance, while dots nearby denote marriage to a wealthy partner. Two small hearts with leaves close by indicate a lover's tiff. If at the bottom of the cup, this can be a health warning.

Horse
The meaning depends upon what the horse is doing. If galloping, this means good news. If there is also a rider, the news comes from afar. A horse's head brings a faithful lover, but clouds around bring delays in romance.

Horseshoe
Good luck, good health, or money coming.

House
If near the handle, there may be domestic trouble. If near the rim, there may be a change of address, but if on the side of the cup, this is temporary. If obscured or at the bottom of the cup, care will be needed at home and at work.

Island
A pleasant vacation.

Jug
If near the rim this means good health, but if near the bottom, this indicates extravagance and losses. Other positions indicate power, prosperity and a position of importance.

Juggler
A good omen for work, but a warning against being taken in by others.

Kettle
If near the handle, comfort and contentment in the home but if accompanied by clouds or at the bottom of the cup, discord and ill health in the home.

Key
A change of address is possible. If double or at the bottom of the cup, a robbery is possible. Crossed keys bring authority and honor in public life, plus success in love. A bunch of keys indicates health, wealth and happiness.

Kite
The questioner is being advised to go ahead with plans but to keep a realistic attitude.

Knife
Quarrels and separations. If near the handle, this seems to be relationship or family matter, but if away from the handle, there may be a stab in the back at work. At the bottom of the cup, problematic legal problems. Otherwise there might be surgery, injections and dental treatment. Crossed knives indicate violence while a broken knife suggests helplessness.

Knight in armor
A helpful man, or a new lover for a female questioner.

Ladder
Spiritual enlightenment and advancement at work. If rungs are missing, there will be setbacks, but if at the bottom of the cup, financial misfortune.

Lamp
Success, financial improvement, celebrations. Two lamps signify two marriages.

Luggage
A journey or even emigration.

Man
If facing toward the handle this denotes a visitor, and if he had his arm stretched out, he will bring gifts. If facing away from the handle, the man could be leaving. If he is shown carrying bags, he is a hard-working man.

Maypole
Fertility. This also indicates that spring will bring improvements.

Monk
A time for rest, retreat and contemplation.

Moon
(See *Crescent*)

Mountains
Obstacles, but if the peaks are clear the questioner will overcome them. With dots, financial success through hard work.

Mouse
Poverty, theft (especially if at the bottom of the cup). Missed opportunities.

Mushroom
A variety of meanings, including setbacks in business, expansion of the questioner's horizons, a home in the country and illusion.

Necklace
Love ties will be important and successful as long as the necklace is complete.

Oak tree
Strength, courage and building something that will last. Happy marriage.

Owl
Gossip, scandal and allegations.

Parachute
A lucky escape.

Parcel
A surprise.

Peacock
With a spread tail, buying land or property. If the image is clear of obstacles, this means luck in marriage, health, wealth and happiness for the questioner and his children. If at the bottom of the cup or obscured, disappointment from children, and plans not working out.

Phoenix
Recovery, rebirth.

Pipe
Problems will be solved. Also a kind and loving man.

Pistol
Danger.

Policeman
Help from those in authority.

Poppy
Loss, sadness, sickness. If near the rim, there will be a rapid recovery.

Pyramid
Achievements, but they will need to be worked at.

Question mark
Caution will be necessary.

Rainbow
Happiness and prosperity. Check where the rainbow ends to see where this applies.

Rat
Treachery, deceit, and loss.

Raven
Bad news, losses, sickness, sadness.

Ring
If complete, a wedding or a happy marriage.

Road
If the road is clear and direct, the future outlook is pleasant and easy but if it is blocked, there will be problems. A fork in the road denotes choices.

Robin
An ancient symbol of death—so there may be a change of circumstances as a result of someone's death.

Rose
Success in creative enterprises, love, happy marriage. If at the bottom of the cup, some delays.

Scaffold
A warning to stay within the limits of the law.

Scales
Lawsuits. If the scales are balanced the legal matters will turn out well; otherwise there will be loss and injustice.

Scepter
Honors and rewards.

Scissors
A separation, quarrels, and misunderstandings.

Shell
Good news, luck and money. Luck in love and justice in legal affairs. A sign of re-birth or a change in consciousness.

Ship
A journey will be lucky, especially if connected to business.

Signpost
See which symbol it points to, as this will be especially important.

Skeleton
Losses, the loss of a friend, or skeletons emerging from the closet.

Soldier

A powerful friend, but alternatively this could indicate hostility towards the questioner.

Spade

Hard work followed by a successful result.

Square

Restriction and hardship, but also protection from real harm.

Stairs

A rise in status at work and in other areas of life.

Star

A six-pointed star indicates good fortune, while a five-pointed one increases spiritual awareness. Small stars close to the handle denote talented children while a large number of stars can denote sadness and loss, although finances would be unaffected. A single star at the bottom of the cup suggests that a change of direction is needed.

Sticks

Crossed sticks indicate quarrels and partings while leaves clustered around a stick indicate bad news. Dots or small leaves nearby suggest that someone will help financially and a ring nearby indicates a marriage.

Sun

Happiness, success, power, and influence. If the sun is obscured, pride will bring a downfall.

Swallow

A change for the better in every way. If close to the handle, the home life will improve, if far from the handle, it foretells a successful and happy trip.

Swan

Progress and contentment, but other possibilities include an interesting lover and an improvement in finances. If the swan is at the bottom of the cup, death or separation.

Sword

(See *Knife*)

Table

Celebrations, meetings, new friends, and discussions of all kinds.

Tower

If the tower is whole, the questioner is building something that will last. If it is incomplete, there will be failures or a change of direction.

Train

A fortunate journey.

Tree

Recovery from sickness, ambitions fulfilled.

Umbrella
If the umbrella is open, there may be a new home. If closed, the questioner may not be able to have it. If inside out, the questioner is responsible for his own problems.

Unicorn
A secret marriage.

Van
Business travel or deliveries, packages arriving, or a move of premises.

Vase
A friend will need the questioner's help.

Violin
Popularity, success, fun and entertainment.

Volcano
Passion or arguments—or both.

Wall
A time to overcome obstacles and build for the future.

Web
Being caught up in an embarrassing or awkward situation.

Whale
Success in a large project.

Wheel
Progress and changes for the better. Success, travel and achievements. If at the bottom of the cup, the questioner must curb impulsiveness.

Wolf
Jealousy and swindles. This can be a lucky sign if the questioner's children are sick, as it denotes recovery for them.

Woman
If the symbol is clear, there will be harmony and happiness but if obscured there may be a jealous or spiteful woman around.

Yacht
An easier life, possibly due to retirement.

Zebra
Travel, possibly even a wandering lifestyle. The questioner may soon have a secret love affair, which will be pleasant—as long as it remains a secret.

WITCH DOCTORS' BONES

Some years ago a friend brought me a small witch doctors' kit of the type that is sold in tourist shops in South Africa. This contained two bones that had clearly once been part of a chicken's leg and four small ones that had been part of the poor chicken's feet; also several small semi-precious stones and two large seeds. Several years later I visited South Africa myself and I treated myself to another set. People occasionally ask me to throw the bones as a party entertainment, and when I do so I find that they work extremely well. These tourist packs are a smaller version of exactly the same kind of bone, stone and seed kit that real Sangomas (witch doctors or shamans) use. The bones appear to work partly by a system that designates a meaning to each bone, stone or seed and partly by opening the Reader up to clairvoyant impressions.

The bones

The larger of the two leg bones represents a male figure and the smaller one represents a female figure. The four small bones can represent children or creative ventures. Two of the stones are brick-red pieces of polished jasper, and these are said to denote evil influences, bad luck, sickness and other misfortunes. The two other stones are beautiful golden-brown striped stones that are known as tiger's eye. These are said to show good influences that emanate from the Enquirer himself due to his use of common sense and any efforts that he makes on his own behalf. The two large seeds represent the wisdom of the ancients, which can be good influences from ancestors and spiritual guides or perhaps the collective wisdom of the tribal elders.

The method

The instruction leaflet suggests that two parallel lines about two to three inches apart should be scratched into the ground with a stick. Then the Sangoma sits opposite the Enquirer, makes a small prayer to his spiritual guides, and throws the bones gently onto the ground. Any object that falls inside the two lines represents people and situations that are close to the Enquirer, also current events or those that will take place in the near future. Items that fall outside the lines represent people and situations that are at a distance from the Enquirer or events that are further away into the future. The further away the object, the more distant the time.

I discovered that the best way to read the bones was to start at the upper left hand side and work down to the lower right hand side. I since discovered that this is a common procedure among people who read crystals and stones here in the west.

TAROT CARDS

Tarot cards are no longer the mysterious objects that they once were, although there are still plenty of people who have never consulted a Tarot reader or been given a reading by a friend who knows how to do it. If you have just acquired a Tarot deck and you are new to the system, this is what you do. Shuffle your cards many times in order to remove their newness and also to mix them up well. Before using the cards for the first time, mentally ask for your cards to be sure to give help and guidance to yourself and others and to bring good luck to all who consult them. Once you have done this, try them out for yourself once or twice but then look around for a couple of guinea-pigs to test them out on as soon after this as possible. At this point, it would also be worth scanning your local bookshop or the Internet for a few books on the subject. My own book, *Fortune Telling by Tarot Cards,* is designed for beginners, and the feedback that I have had from this tells me that people find it clear and easy to understand. In the meantime, here is some basic information that will get you off the ground.

The Tarot deck

A Tarot deck is composed of two sections, these being the Major Arcana and the Minor Arcana. The Major Arcana is a set of twenty-two cards that are both powerful and completely individual in that they don't link with any other cards. The Minor Arcana is a set of fifty-six cards that are arranged in four suits, much like a deck of playing cards. (Playing cards evolved from the Tarot.) Each suit contains an Ace, cards that are numbered from two to ten, then a Page, Knight, Queen and King. The suits are called Cups, Wands, Coins and Swords. Some decks use different names, so it is common to find the suit of Wands called Rods or Staves and the suit of Coins called Pentacles, due to the pentacle shaped design on the coins in those decks.

When you have shuffled and laid out the cards, you may notice that some of them are the wrong way up. At this point, I suggest that you simply turn these cards the right way up. Some readers use reversed cards and assign a different meaning to them, which is often a weaker version of the upright card meaning. However many readers only use the cards in the upright position, so I suggest that for the time being you do the same.

The Major Arcana

Many of the powerful Major Arcana cards signify new beginnings, turning points and major events, but it is sometimes difficult to assess what these might be, so it is the Minor Arcana cards that surround these cards that usually throw light on the subject. The ratio of cards in a Tarot deck is two thirds Minor Arcana to less than one third Major Arcana, so if more than one third of the reading contains Major Arcana cards, you can be sure that fate is controlling the person's destiny. If less than a third of the cards in a reading are Major Arcana ones, the chances are that the person is in charge of his own destiny at the time of the reading.

The Minor Arcana

Each suit is related to a different aspect of life. Cups represent emotional situations or an emotional reaction to something, along with creativity and matters of affection. Wands represent day-to-day activities and such things as one's job, communicating with others, dealing with minor hassles, travel, household issues, and all the usual running around and coping with life that we all have to do. Coins represent resources, and these may signify income, finance, property, land, a farm, a business, a career and practical matters as a whole. Swords represent ideas and the need to take action, and often problem areas that are likely to arise.

It makes sense to assess the nature of the cards that turn up in a reading. For instance, if Cup cards dominate, you can be sure that the person's feelings about a situation will be paramount, and the reading itself may well concern romance, love and relationships. If Wands dominate, then the person will be very busy. If Coins are the issue, then practical matters and such things as job security, finances, the value of a property or something else of the kind is in the air. If Swords dominate a reading, storm clouds may be gathering and some kind of action needs to be taken.

When teaching the Tarot, I often tell this little story. A person becomes fed up with his job and decides that he must look for something else (problems, action = Swords). He scans the newspaper and the Internet and asks friends if they know of any jobs that might be going (communication, activity = Wands). The person finds a good job that is in the right area and that pays well (practical matters, finances = Coins). When he starts the job he soon finds that he is very comfortable and happy there or that it doesn't really suit him—despite the fact that the job appears to be what he wants (feelings, sensitivity to surroundings or people = Cups).

The Court cards

Generally speaking, the King and Queen cards represent people in a reading. The Knights also represent people, but they can also indicate movement in one's affairs. The Pages tend to represent young people or those who are less important to the questioner, but they often represent news and communications of various kinds. There are various ways of categorizing the Court cards, but the following makes life easy for a beginner:

- Kings signify mature men, Queens signify mature women, Knights signify younger men and the Pages signify younger women and children.
- Cups indicate emotional people who may be loving, easily upset or short-tempered and they often represent people who affect our emotions.
- Wands represent friendly, competent people who communicate well and who are good to work with. They may have teaching ability, logic and wisdom, but they may not be as passionate as we would like them to be.
- Coins denote practical people who can give us financial advice or fix things that are broken. They have great resources and much common sense but they may be a little dull when it comes to love and romance.
- Swords suggest exciting people who may stimulate us on an intellectual level or a sexual one, but they have an innate aggression or instability that can make life difficult for us. These people are wonderful to consult when professional or specialist advice is required and they can represent such types as doctors, lawyers and other professionals in our lives when this is appropriate.

If you are into astrology, here is another idea for you to play with. Cup cards represent water sign people, Wand cards represent fire or air sign people, Coin cards represent earth sign people, and Sword cards also represent fire or air sign people. Even if these cards don't actually link to a person's sun sign element (although they often do), they can express the character of those elements.

Spreads and layouts

There are many Tarot spreads, but as a beginner I suggest that you experiment with the following two ideas. The first will suit those of you who have a more intuitive approach, while the second will suit those who need more guidance or a more logical approach. There is no either/or situation here, you can try using both techniques. Both systems start off the same way.

Ask your questioner to shuffle the cards and then give them back to you. Now lay out seven cards from the top of the deck and place them in a row in front of you. Note whether there are more than two Major Arcana cards, as this will tell you that your questioner is in the hands of fate. Note which suit of the Minor Arcana predominates as this will tell you whether you are looking at an emotional situation, a financial or practical one, a fairly ordinary one or something really difficult. See if there are any Court cards, because if these predominate, it shows that other people are a major factor in the life of your Questioner.

If you want to take an intuitive approach, simply look at the cards again and read them one by one from left to right, using the interpretations in this book. You can even use this as a crude timing device, as the first couple of cards will probably show the current situation, while the later one show how things will develop.

To make the second system work, you need to take eight small pieces of paper. Now write the word "relationships" on one piece of paper and put this down on the table. Write the word "money" on the second piece of paper and place that on your table. Now do the same for the other six, writing the words "health," "family," "property," "career," "other interests" and "potluck."

At this stage, you will have to ask your questioner what his other interests might be. A professional reader will be expected to pick up everything that is on a client's mind from the cards, but you can be forgiven for asking. Your questioner may tell you that he is having problems with a neighbor or he may be in desperate need of a new car. He may be interested in some sport or hobby, he may have a journey on his mind or he may be concerned about any one of a hundred other things. Once you know what this is, you will be able to apply the card to the reading. The potluck card will probably throw up something that neither of you has considered.

Now lay your seven cards out by placing each card above each piece of paper and read each card in the context of the situation that it falls into. For instance, if a card that talks of property matters falls in the property area, you can be sure that there will be a change of address or a positive outcome to a property matter. However, if it falls in a romantic or work area, then it is likely that a property, home, premises or place has some relevance to the reading. If this turns up in the pot-luck section, then the questioner may not be concerned about a property matter at the time of the reading—but this may become an issue in his future.

If after this, you want more information on any matter, simply ask your questioner to shuffle the cards again and read seven cards by the intuitive method but apply the whole seven-card layout to the specific question or situation. For instance, if you have picked up on a question of love and you want more information, a reading that is devoted to love alone will probably give you the answer.

Interpreting the cards

In some cases, I offer more than one potential interpretation but these are necessarily brief in this book. My books *Fortune Telling by Tarot Cards* and *Super Tarot* will give you much deeper meanings and many more alternative ideas than I can offer here. *Super Tarot* will show you how to overcome the problem that all beginners face, which is how to link the cards together to obtain a sensible and coherently synthesized reading. My other books offer meanings for reversed cards, but I only interpret their upright meanings here.

The suit of Cups

Ace of Cups
The beginning of love, affection and friendship. A gift, perhaps a ring. Joyful news, possibly the birth of a child.

Two of Cups
A successful relationship or happy partnership, possibly also a reconciliation.

Three of Cups
A wedding, either for the questioner or for someone he cares about. Celebration, joy, childbirth, parties and fun.

Four of Cups
Dissatisfaction because the questioner may want more than he can have. This may be friendship when what he really wants is love. To some extent, a search for something new.

Five of Cups
Loss and sadness, but something remains from which the questioner can begin to rebuild his life.

Six of Cups
Past skills and past associations will have meaning or become useful again in the future. Family gatherings and catching up with old contacts. Also contact with children or revisiting one's own childhood in some way.

Seven of Cups
There are many options on offer but the questioner needs to use both logic and intuition to work out which is likely to be the best. If money is a stumbling block to romance, this will soon be overcome.

Eight of Cups
The end of a miserable time is in sight. Soon the questioner will turn his back on past problems and move slowly forward.

Nine of Cups
Great satisfaction, but the questioner must guard against smugness. Possibly marriage to a mature person.

Ten of Cups
Joy, happiness, happy family life. A birth is possible.

Page of Cups
A gentle, loving and sensitive young woman or child. A time to study and reflect. Business matters will proceed slowly but surely.

Knight of Cups
A kindly, good-natured young man but he may be immature. Even an older man can be indicated here, but he will be ruled by immature emotions. Changes in relationships. A lover may travel soon. Slow changes in affairs.

Queen of Cups
A loving and very feminine woman brings love and comfort. She is kind and generous but may be materialistic and lazy.

King of Cups
A kindly, emotional man who cares for the questioner. He has a complex character that makes him exciting but he can be dogmatic, difficult and dictatorial. He is sensual, loving, and fond of children and of the good life.

The suit of Wands

Ace of Wands
The birth of an idea, a child, new possibilities, a rebirth of some kind.

Two of Wands
A partnership or relationship that is based on shared interests. Sometimes this indicates a move or perhaps a proud man who is around the questioner.

Three of Wands
New projects, a new job, and good news. There may be travel in connection with work. Partnerships and relationships work well.

Four of Wands
Security and a feeling of putting down roots, and sometimes this refers to a new house with a bit of land around it.

Five of Wands
Challenges, but these can be dealt with successfully and even enjoyably. Courage will be needed. Travel plans may be put on hold.

Six of Wands
Victory, achievement, earning a living. Problems will be overcome, delays will be ended and legal matters will succeed.

Seven of Wands
There is much to do, but if the questioner takes one thing at a time in a logical order, he will succeed. There may be temporary problems relating to health, money, obstructive people or other situations but they will soon pass.

Eight of Wands
Travel and new experiences will broaden the questioner's horizons. Friendship and even love may be on the way.

Nine of Wands
The questioner is now in a reasonably secure situation but he must stay alert. Most problems are behind him but he should remain prudent for a while longer.

Ten of Wands
There are many burdens and responsibilities but the effort is worthwhile.

Page of Wands
A bright and rather restless child. A journey, visitors, letters and phone calls. Writing could be important soon. Property matters will go smoothly.

Knight of Wands

A friendly and intelligent man. An interest in communications work or there may be contact with teachers. Visitors, house moves, travel and correspondence. A lively atmosphere.

Queen of Wands

A charming, clever woman who is a good companion, perhaps a clever businesswoman with a mind of her own. She may lack confidence, rush into things or get irritated when hassled. She is sexy, loving, and a good friend.

King of Wands

An attractive man with a ready smile. Amusing and interesting, he is a good communicator and teacher. Helpful in a working relationship but a bit detached emotionally.

The suit of Coins

Ace of Coins

There is money coming or perhaps a new source of income. There may be a win, a bonus, or a raise in salary or status. Good news regarding money or a fresh start where funds and resources are concerned.

Two of Coins

A separation of resources. This may involve juggling time or money or borrowing to pay for something. Alternatively, putting money aside for some purpose or a division of funds due to divorce or a separation.

Three of Coins

Buying or renovating a property. Being given a job or a project to do. Using skills successfully and perhaps a fresh start connected to work or some project.

Four of Coins

Financial stability, stable resources, security. Perhaps too much emphasis on money for the questioner's good.

Five of Coins

Loss, delays in payment, examination failure. Sometimes love goes well but finance is worrisome for a while.

Six of Coins

Money can be paid out or shared out. The questioner will be able to repay debts, finance a divorce or help others who are worse off. He must guard against being drained by others.

Seven of Coins

Slow growth and steady achievement. Work that brings satisfaction and perhaps also monetary gain.

Eight of Coins
A new job, much work to be done, a creative endeavor, or a new skill to be learned.

Nine of Coins
Money and success are on the way. A good time to buy goods for the home or to start growing things. Home life will be happy.

Ten of Coins
Money, success, and pleasure from personal achievement. Travel in connection with work. A good marriage and happy family life. Setting up something that will last. A successful business.

Page of Coins
A steady, practical, business-like youngster. Good news about money or travel. Promotion or success, especially for young people around the questioner.

Knight of Coins
A cautious young or immature man. News about business, money, or practical matters. Travel in connection with work.

Queen of Coins
A practical, businesslike woman. A skilled negotiator and good homemaker. A loving companion, albeit that she is rather materialistic.

King of Coins
A solid citizen, a financial advisor. A cautious and sensible man who needs financial and emotional security but may be somewhat tight-fisted. A kindly family man.

The suit of Swords

Ace of Swords
A new idea and perhaps a fresh start. A situation that needs thought and effort. Deep feelings will be aroused, possibly with some passion. Power and justice will be on the way soon.

Two of Swords
Stalemate. No change yet. The questioner can't see where he is going yet.

Three of Swords
Loss, sadness, sickness, and blood.

Four of Swords
Rest and recuperation, recovery from illness or worries. Possibly a connection with a hospital, health clinic, dentist, or therapist that is due to the questioner's work or for a good purpose.

Five of Swords
Quarrels, jealousy and partings. The questioner will need to stand up for himself, and perhaps also to accept a parting. Someone may leave the questioner's circle.

Six of Swords

Travel over water, a journey that may bring a turning point. Moving into a new environment, moving away from trouble, even becoming some kind of refugee. A gradual improvement in circumstances.

Seven of Swords

The questioner needs to move on, taking what he can and leaving what he cannot take or use in the future. This may be a literal move or a metaphorical one. Legal advice may be needed. In some circumstances this may indicate a robbery or fraud.

Eight of Swords

The questioner or some aspect of his life is temporarily tied down and he cannot see how to escape. Perhaps he chooses to stay stuck.

Nine of Swords

Illness, worry and family problems. Sometimes an issue related to mothers or motherhood is a cause of worry. Often the problems are less serious than they appear to be and the questioner is advised to do something rather than dwell on them.

Ten of Swords

Treachery and betrayal, a stab in the back. Loss, death, divorce, the end of a situation, a collapse of plans.

Page of Swords

An active, sporty, intelligent child. The questioner should keep his eyes open as there may be important events going on. News of an opportunity or news of an unexpected problem. A contract or document. Advice, possibly given in secret.

Knight of Swords

A tough, brave and intelligent young man. However, he may be aggressive or rash. Arguments and disputes. Decisions that need to be taken. Medical or legal matters to be faced, or perhaps a journey that needs to be made on the spur of the moment.

Queen of Swords

A clever, sharp woman who may be highly qualified. She demands respect and can give cool professional advice. Alternatively, a woman may be aggressive, hurtful, sarcastic, jealous or untrustworthy.

King of Swords

A clever and well-qualified man or one who can fix things. Help from a specialist of some kind. Alternatively, an aggressive, unpleasant man.

The Major Arcana

These are stand-alone cards. They each have a basic meaning and also far deeper implications than I have room for in this book. If one Major Arcana card confuses you, try taking another card from the deck and see if the combination of two cards can offer more information.

0.
The Fool
A new chapter is about to open up, and this may take the questioner into unfamiliar territory. Whatever it happens to be, the questioner will be will be spiritually protected.

1.
The Magician
The questioner is about to tackle something new, but this is not something that is so far out of his experience that it leaves him floundering. He has the skills and experience to do this. This can sometimes indicate self-employment or the start of a business, but it could apply to spiritual work or indeed, any other kind of matter. This can indicate the arrival of an important new man in a woman's reading.

2.
The High Priestess
This stands for a mental approach where emotions can only cloud the issue. A combination of brains and intuition will be needed. Teaching or studying may become important and an instructor or advisor may turn up when he or she is wanted. For those who work in a spiritual field, this indicates that there is more work to come or that a practical job will need a spiritual slant.

3.
The Empress
There will be fruitfulness and abundance, fulfillment and contentment. The questioner can look forward to a happy marriage and children. Sometimes this indicates a move to a nice place that has some land around it. There will be emotional and financial security. Sometimes a mother figure proves to be helpful.

4.
The Emperor
The questioner will soon be in control of his situation and he may achieve a position of power either at work or within the family. Sometimes this refers to a boss, a father figure or to the man in a woman's life, and if so this person should be reliable and successful.

5.
The Hierophant
A teacher, guru or spiritual advisor may soon help the questioner. Advice and help will be forthcoming. The questioner is advised to avoid anything illegal or dangerous and to keep to the traditional, straight and narrow path. It would be best if the questioner sticks to convention and tradition in the future.

6.

The Lovers

This card often indicates that some kind of choice needs to be made and it is important for the questioner to bear in mind that the outcome of his decision will affect those around him. Love affairs and relationships will soon be important. A working partnership or cooperative venture will succeed. The questioner will soon improve his dress and appearance and make his surroundings attractive.

7.

The Chariot

The questioner has some kind of battle or project on his hands, but he should be able to deal with this successfully. Sometimes this card refers to travel or to the purchase or maintenance of a vehicle.

8.

Justice

In some decks, the Justice card is placed in the number eleven position, in others it is number eight as it is shown here. The meaning is quite simple, because it shows that justice, fair play and a balanced outcome is the right one. If the questioner has a legal matter or any other matter where a fair outcome is needed, this will occur. Balance must be sought.

9.

The Hermit

This indicates that the questioner needs to take some time out from the hustle and bustle of daily life and do some thinking. He needs to retreat and reflect in order to obtain a clearer picture of what is needed.

10.

The Wheel of Fortune

This one is simple because all it means is that a change is on the way. If you lay out your row of cards and count them off as weeks or months, the position that this card falls in will show you when the change will come about.

11.

Strength

This card appears as number eight in some decks rather than as number eleven as it is shown here. If the questioner is sick, he will soon be feeling much better. If he has been in a weak position, this will also change for the better. This card implies gentle strength rather than aggression—so tact, diplomacy, a calm attitude and a certain amount of endurance will be required.

12.

The Hanged Man

The first meaning for this complex card is suspension. The questioner may be anxious for something to happen immediately, but when this card shows up, the chances are that he will have to wait a while longer. The second meaning is of sacrifice, in the sense that in order to for one to have one thing, another needs to be sacrificed. For instance, the questioner may have to give up some of his free time in order to get something done. A third meaning is that of initiation, in the sense that nobody can understand someone else's problems until they have been through something similar themselves. Therefore, in its way, this is a card of enlightenment.

13.

Death

This is the dreaded death card that frightens those who are new to the Tarot. In my experience it never foretells the death of the questioner, although it can indicate the death of someone around him if appropriate. However, its true meaning is that of transformation, in the sense that nothing stays the same forever. If the questioner is wondering whether something is coming to a conclusion or whether something is really over, the answer is that it is—and that there will be no road back.

14.

Temperance

This card talks of moderation in all things and of a time of peace. There will be a good balance between the various sides of the questioner's life and for once everything will go well.

15.

The Devil

This is another card that frightens newcomers to the Tarot, but it denotes bondage to something that is outmoded or that is no longer really valid. Unpleasant emotions like jealousy, rage, guilt, hanging on to the past or to a situation that is no longer working are all issues that need to be addressed. A practical rather than an emotional attitude will be needed. There may be a commitment to something healthy, such as a mortgage or a period of study, but the implications must be considered. Spiritual enlightenment may be on the way soon.

No. 16.

The Tower

Some decks call this The Struck Tower, and it is another unpleasant card. It frequently suggests that a shock or upheaval is on the way, and as this is likely to be unexpected, it can take some dealing with. Whether the upset is large or small, it can't be ignored. Sometimes there is an element of enlightenment, as at least the questioner will know what has been going on, which means that he can do something about it. The Tower is a structure, so this card can refer to a problem that concerns the structure of the questioner's home or business premises.

No. 17.

The Star

This is often called The Star of Hope, as it foretells a better time ahead when hopes and wishes will come true. The questioner may learn something new or become wiser in the future. It can indicate study, travel or widening of horizons.

18.

The Moon

The questioner is being faced with a situation where he cannot see daylight, or where he cannot see the forest for the trees. Nothing is clear and it is hard for him to make reasoned judgements. In romantic matters, it shows that nothing is what it seems. In any circumstance, lies, half-truths and mysteries abound. Sometimes this indicates a problem for a mother figure.

19.

The Sun

This is a card of joy and success. A love affair will go well, a marriage will be happy, a business venture will succeed. If appropriate, the questioner will pass an exam or a test of some kind. Children and anything that relates to them will bring joy and happiness.

20.

Judgement

The questioner will be rewarded for his efforts. If he has been struggling with something for a while, it will work out to his satisfaction. He will be rewarded for past work and he will feel content with himself. Ideas and projects that have been shelved will come alive soon.

21.

The World

Something is working its way to a conclusion and there will soon be space and time for something new to take its place. Sometimes this is a card of travel and expansion of horizons. Sometimes it just means that a phase of life will reach its natural conclusion, in readiness for something new.

PREDICTIVE ASTROLOGY

Astrology is a massive subject and the horoscopes you see in a newspaper or magazine are only the tip of a huge iceberg. You can be sure that the astrologer who writes the column knows a great deal, although little of this is reflected by what you see in the paper. Astrology can be used as an incredibly accurate form of psychoanalysis, for assessing the viability of love relationships, business partnerships, and political regimes, and for picking the best time to start a project or to track the outcome of an illness. Astrology is not hard to learn and anyone can get a grasp of the basics quite quickly. However, if you want to become a proficient you will need to take some courses and buy books and computer software that will enable you to produce modern horoscope charts. Having said all that, here is a quick overview of the way that predictive astrology works.

Newspaper astrology

Newspapers and magazines work on the only method that is possible when dealing with readers who don't know what their rising signs are or where their natal planets are situated. This method is called "sun sign astrology" or "solar house astrology" because the sign that the sun appears in at birth is treated as the first astrological "house." The following illustrations show the solar house arrangements for people born under the signs of Taurus and Aquarius. The

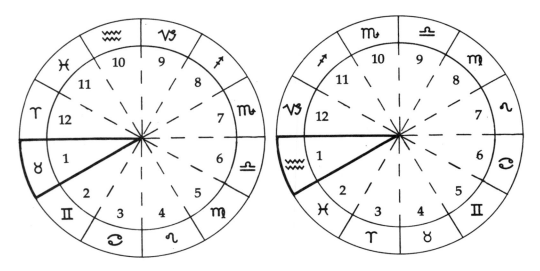

Signs used as Houses

signs of the zodiac are always arranged in an anti-clockwise direction around the chart, and the first house is always on the left hand side, as shown in the illustrations.

The signs of the zodiac are always written in the same order with Aries being the first sign and Pisces being the last.

Symbol	Sign
♈	Aries
♉	Taurus
♊	Gemini
♋	Cancer
♌	Leo
♍	Virgo
♎	Libra
♏	Scorpio
♐	Sagittarius
♑	Capricorn
♒	Aquarius
♓	Pisces

The signs of the Zodiac

The sun has a regular pattern with the only variation being the exact time or date upon which it changes from one sign to the next during any particular year. This predictability means that even a non-astrologer can make a start on predicting his future trends. This is where the sun will be during any year (with minor variations at the cusp of each sign).

March 21 to April 19	Aries
April 20 to May 20	Taurus
May 21 to June 21	Gemini
June 22 to July 22	Cancer
July 23 to August 22	Leo
August 23 to September 22	Virgo
September 23 to October 23	Libra
October 24 to November 21	Scorpio
November 22 to December 21	Sagittarius
December 22 to January 19	Capricorn
January 20 to February 18	Aquarius
February 19 to March 20	Pisces

During the course of a year, the sun moves through all twelve signs, while the moon does this during the course of a lunar month. Mercury and Venus are close to the sun, which means that either or both these planets can be found in the same sign, or either planet can be one sign ahead or behind. The other planets have varying orbits, ranging from Mars, which spends a few weeks in each sign, to Pluto, which spends an average of twenty years in each sign. Therefore, the only way to discover where your planets were at birth or where they have moved to at any point in your life is to consult an astrologer, send off for a computerized astrology printout, or learn astrology yourself.

Easy predicting

Using the system that the newspapers employ, draw a circle and divide it into twelve "houses," with the first one on the left side as shown earlier in this chapter. Put your sun sign in the first house and write all the other signs in order around the side in an counter-clockwise direction. Therefore, if your sign is Gemini, that will be your first solar house, Cancer will be your second house, Leo your third, and so on until you reach Taurus, which will be your twelfth house.

Now it is a matter of working out which house the sun will be in during any month of the year. Once you have done that, consult the interpretation below to see what happens when the sun appears to move through any one of your houses. Naturally, there is far more to predictive astrology than this, but this is something that you can do for yourself without studying astrology at all.

The first house
The testosterone level rises.
This represents a fresh start, the beginning of something new or simply a more optimistic attitude. If you have been hanging back from something, you will take matters into your own hands and put things into action. This is a very masculine house, so it shows assertion—but also such things as speed, male-dominated jobs or tasks, and political ambition.

The second house
What's it worth to me?
The second house concerns anything that is of value to a person. This may mean money, income, resources and personal possessions, but it also relates to the lifestyle that a person values, his main priorities and also his self-image. To some extent this rules love and relationships, especially when land, property, farming and goods are involved in the equation. This house is associated with artistic and musical interests and any attraction to work or the world of beauty, fashion and glamour.

The third house

Talk, talk, talk.

This house signifies the ability to learn, speak, write, deal with foreign languages, communicate, and negotiate with others. It rules messages, errands, and the panoply of modern machinery that is involved with information technology. In addition, it is concerned with a subject's vehicle or any other means of local travel. Neighbors, siblings, and young people, such as nephews and nieces, and some friendships are shown here, as are sports, games and youthful occupations.

The fourth house

Home is where the mortgage is.

This rules the home and property, including a person's business premises. It symbolizes domestic life, the roots, background, family history, and security. This relates to the mother, any mother figure and family commitments. It can rule females in general and female products or services, and has a connection with the feminine aspect of giving help and service to others. It can rule tasks that involve dealing with the public.

The fifth house

Creating anything, including havoc.

Children and their education are found here, as are fun, holidays, games and leisure pursuits, including some sports, dancing, singing, writing, and entertainment—especially if it contains a touch of glamour. This house denotes creativity and bringing things into being, including childbirth and business enterprises. Even publishing can be seen here if the person uses it to make a personal statement. Flirtation and love affairs that are meant to be fun can be seen here.

The sixth house

Work and health.

This house is associated with our daily work and daily chores. It also relates to the whole business of employing people and being employed, and the services that we perform for others. This is different from the tenth house, which may also relate to the career. However, the tenth house would be in the sense of the status and wealth that this brings, rather than the actual functions that we perform in our daily lives. Health matters are still very much concerned with the sixth house.

The seventh house

Love and hate.

This house rules open relationships such as marriage, partnerships, and working partnerships. Legal arrangements, cooperation, and pulling together are signified here. However, this house also rules open enemies. This is concerned with beauty, art, music, leisure, lovemaking, and pleasure.

The eighth house

Hatch, match, and dispatch.

The eighth house is also connected to the idea of partnership but in a more serious manner because it rules shared resources, shared financial matters, legally binding business arrangements, and union of all kinds. Thus sex and resultant childbirth can be shown here—as can death. This house rules anything that is hidden from view, including secrets, crime, interests that are not broadcasts to others, and anything that really is under the ground, such as coal, oil, gold and other such resources. This house represents crime and investigation, forensic matters, and also cutting and gouging, as in surgery or even butchery.

The ninth house

To boldly go.

This house expands a person's horizons, so it is concerned with further or higher education, foreign travel, foreign goods or foreign people. Also exploring legal boundaries, searching for the truth of a matter and exploring religious, philosophical and spiritual ideas. It is about discovering what a person needs to believe in.

The tenth house

The ladder of success.

If you have drawn the design properly, you will see that this house starts at the top of the chart, therefore it rules a person's aims and aspirations. It is often taken to mean the job or career, but it really means the search for status and position in any sphere—even if this means having a more impressive television than the neighbors. This rules achievements, fame, public acclaim, and sometimes public disgrace. It is concerned with fathers and father figures.

The eleventh house

Detached relationships.

This is the house of acquaintanceship, friendship, group activities, clubs and partying with friends. It rules intellectual pursuits and hobbies and original ideas or inventions. It can apply to teaching and learning, especially if the person is exploring ideas rather than getting a basic education. The eleventh house rules eccentricity, but also desire for change and even for revolution. It is especially associated with unexpected events and sudden upheavals. It can refer to stepchildren and adopted children.

The twelfth house
The inner world.

This rules a person's private place and his inner thoughts and feelings. It encompasses such things as fears, sorrows, and self-undoing, but it also rules a love of art, music, and creativity. Hidden talents, hidden lovers, and much else that is not obvious to outsiders are tucked away here. This house represents escapism—sometimes into alcohol or drug addiction, but also places of seclusion, such as hospitals, prisons, a monk's cell, and the shed at the bottom of one's garden. However, along with such unpleasant matters as karmic debts, it also rules kindness and good deeds both given and received, especially if this is done quietly.

PALMISTRY

My friend Jonathan Dee has had his own radio astrology show for many years, so he is very well known in his area. Jon can read Tarot cards and much else, but he is not a hand reader. Many times when Jon is enjoying a quiet drink with friends at his favorite bar, some idiot will come up to him and ask if he is *the* Jon Dee. Upon receiving a polite yes, the idiot will aggressively thrust out his hand, while at the same time looking over his shoulder and smirking in the direction of his mates to show them how bold and clever he is. This gets the idiot nowhere. Firstly, there is no earthly reason why an off-duty fortune teller should read anything—especially when the request comes in such an insulting manner. Secondly, brilliant as Jon Dee undoubtedly is . . . he can't read hands!

This fact frequently astonishes members of the public (and not only idiots in bars), because it is the most universally understood method of fortune telling, and it may well be the oldest. Hand reading is not an easy subject to pick up in the way that some other divinations are. It takes years of study to become even an adequate hand reader, and a lifetime to become a really good one.

The following pages will give you an introduction to the art of hand reading but you need to buy several books and then look at as many hands as you can and then to check your findings with their owners.

The three major lines

The illustration (Fig. 1) shows the heart line, the head line, and the life line.

The life line

A strong life line shows health, strength, and the ability to bounce back from illness, but it doesn't necessarily show the length of life. A short or broken life line (Fig. 2) often "moves" across to some other part of the hand. This indicates a major change in life, such as divorce, emigration, major career changes and much else. A lifeline that clings around the thumb shows a home-loving person who prefers a stable job that keeps him in one place and a desire to put family life first. A life line that travels out across the hand signifies a more adventurous, career-minded person who loves to travel and who needs personal freedom. Forks on the line indicate that the person wants both options (Fig. 3).

Disturbances on the line can indicate health problems and life events—and here is just one example. The illustration (Fig. 4) shows the kind of dots or pits that indicate temporary or permanent spinal problems. If these are close to the

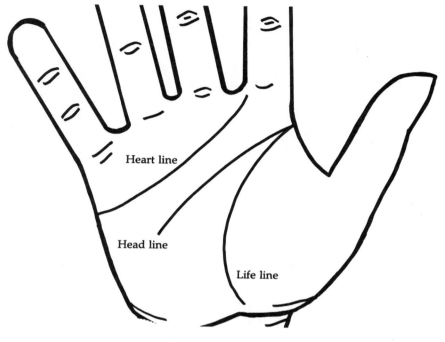

Fig. 1 The major lines

Fig. 2 The life line showing a change of circumstance
The head line bears this out

Fig. 3 Desire for a career and family life

Fig. 4 A painful backache

top of the line, the neck will be affected, if they are closer to the lower end of the line, the lumbar or sacral area will be affected.

Length of life

A person who is destined to live a long life will have at least some lines at the top of the hand, while a person who remains active until the end will have many of these. Take care when reading the hands of young people, because these lines don't all form until well into adulthood—sometimes even later. This shows that a person's fate is not necessarily written in the hand, and that personal choices and changes in circumstances can affect one's destiny.

I have reproduced the following illustration from a print of my mother's hand. Frances Waxman was so active that she carried on doing ballroom and energetic Latin-American dancing with my stepfather right up to about six weeks before her death at the age of eighty-nine!

Lines at the top of the hand

The head line

Some palmists call this the line of intelligence. It shows how the person's mind works, and to some extent the kind of career choice they will make. A short line suggests that the person is either a specialist in his subject or that he has few interests. A line that extends across the hand or that wanders diagonally downwards shows a lively mind and many interests. A horizontal line indicates a logical mind that is suited to practical tasks such as math or computing, while a sloping one is more suited to working for or with others, and that the mind is more open to music, poetry, and romance. Once again, bends, breaks, islands or disturbances on the head line can indicate specific health problems or changes in the career path.

The heart line

This shows the way a person feels, and to some extent the path of his love life. If the line is deep, curving, and bold, the person is able to give and receive love, and while his love life may or may not run smoothly, he will certainly have one! A curved line that reaches up to the fingers belongs to a true romantic who selects his partner almost on impulse and mainly because he loves, desires and is fascinated by that person.

A straight line that runs horizontally across the hand indicates caution. This person chooses a partner based on race, religion, social status, educational background, financial background or for some other practical purpose. This doesn't mean that the subject cannot *love* his chosen partner, but that he would find it hard to go against his mental programming for anything other than a quick fling. Many people have a forked line which shows that they could be attracted to a partner for either of the above reasons, or both.

Attachment lines

A person's attitude toward important relationships, and to some extent the number and progress of his love relationships can be seen on the side of the hand, as per the illustrations below. These used to be called marriage lines but these days any strong attachment will apply.

Attachment lines

- It would be easy to read a person's future if one line meant one partnership, two lines meant two and so on, but this is not quite the case. The following shows you some of the options:
- One strong line shows a person who wants to attach to one person and stay with them for life—and it can mean that they do just that. However, if it cannot be so, they will find someone else and try to do the same with them.
- Two lines suggest that the person will not ignore relationship problems. If they become too severe, the person won't hesitate to leave and start looking around for someone new.

- One strong line, or perhaps two strong lines and one or two weaker ones suggest several potential mates, but only one or two serious ones.
- A young person who is not ready to settle down or someone who tried a relationship but prefers playing the field may have many weak lines. If their circumstances and outlook changes, one of these lines will strengthen and the others will fade away.

Obviously the clearer and cleaner these lines are, the more straightforward the person's situation. Here are a few possibilities:

The course of events

- A clear line (a) denotes a relationship that is basically sound.
- A messy line (b) denotes problems. If the line mends itself later, these will be sorted out.
- A broken line (c) shows parting and coming back together.
- An "island" (d) suggests that the partner is temporarily suffering bad health.
- A fork (f) represents problems that might or might not end in divorce.
- A drooping line (e) shows that the subject's partner is nagging, dominating or bullying the subject.

Child lines

These are difficult to spot, so you need to look for them in a very good light. Try dotting a little talcum powder, face powder or powdered eye-shadow on this area of the hand, as this can help to make these lines clear.

The child lines must cross through at least one attachment line for the child to be part of the subject's life. In theory, one line indicates one child, two lines indicate two children and so on, but a line can also indicate a good relationship with a stepchild so this doesn't always indicate childbirth. Miscarriages and abortions don't usually create a long or strong line, but if the person doesn't forget the lost child, the line can sometimes appear like the line for a living child. Some people have lines but no children. These subjects may look after children or even animals. If there are no child lines, the person may choose not to have children, may not be able to have them, may never have any dealings with children— or children are so far into their future that the lines have not yet formed.

Child lines

The fate line

The fate line runs roughly up the middle of the hand. It is not easy to assess because it can rise from the life line, the bottom of the hand or the side that is away from the thumb. There can be a section of line at the lower end of the hand that peters out later or one that only starts fairly high up the hand.

The fate line can run towards the index finger as in the first illustration or towards the middle finger, as per the second illustration. It rarely runs to the ring finger but it can throw branches in that direction. If it rises from the life line, as per the second illustration, the subject's

The fate line

Problems

family will help him to make a good start in life. If from the outer (percussion) side of the hand, other people will help him.

- A long straight fate line suggests a well-defined fate and a person who does his duty according to the society that he lives in, but he may never strike out for independence or discover who or what he really is.
- A messy line with breaks, branches, accompanying lines, islands, bars across it and deviations of any kind represent a more interesting but less secure lifestyle.
- A fate line that starts early and then peters out shows a change of direction and perhaps a less defined sense of direction after the line ends.
- A fate line that starts late suggests that it will take time before the person has a clear idea of where he wants to go in life.
- A fate line that travels towards the index finger suggests determination, ambition, self-belief, and success in life.
- A fate line that travels towards the middle finger suggests that the person needs to work hard in order to provide for himself and others, but that success and a high level of status can be achieved.
- The line rarely goes in the direction of the ring finger, but if it throws a branch in that direction, the person can expect a nice home and a good deal of fun later in life.
- Islands on the line indicate times of confusion, financial problems, relationship troubles, and possible periods of ill health.
- Breaks denote breaks in the run of a person's life. If the line breaks and jumps to the thumb side, a change of career can be indicated. If it jumps to the percussion side, the person may pay less attention to a career or even give up work in order to concentrate on home life.

- Lines that join the fate line denote major influences in the person's life. This can indicate lovers, marriage partners, business partners, or indeed anybody who has an impact on his life.
- Parallel lines or a long island on the line show that the person's resources and energies are split—often between work and family or some other consideration.

Here are two more common scenarios:

Self-employed

The career stops and family life takes over

Needless to say, there is much more to palmistry than this, and every single part of the hand, including the back of the hand and the finger nails has a story to tell. Hands are also wonderful maps to a subject's state of health, state of mind, and his life as a whole.

If this tiny introduction to this fascinating subject leaves you wanting more, seek out books on the subject. A little later this year, look around for my book *Modern Palmistry*.

The real thing